I KNOW THIS MUCH IS TRUE

I Know This Much is True

A Collection of Essays & Thoughts on Life

S. KILATA

Wanderlust Mystic

This book is for Raylan, Anabel, & Kaylie...the humans who have taught me more about life than anyone else. Watching you grow into adulthood has been my biggest joy, and I am beyond proud of each of you for honoring your individualities.

Note to Reader:
This book explores themes around generational trauma, sexual abuse, and addiction.

CONTENTS

DEDICATION - v

Liminal

1

~ 1 ~

something bigger than yourself

2

~ 2 ~

momma | 2020

4

~ 3 ~

a whole new life | 2001

6

~ 4 ~

easter service | 2003

9

~ 5 ~

hollie hobbie | 1982

11

~ 6 ~
lot's daughters | 2019
14

~ 7 ~
come as you are | 2009
17

~ 8 ~
myrtle neck, part one | 1976
20

~ 9 ~
demerol | 2005
24

~ 10 ~
cry it out, part one | 2018
26

~ 11 ~
there was a time you wouldn't have put up with this shit | 2019
29

~ 12 ~
cry it out, part two | 2022
36

~ 13 ~
a golden chord | 2020
39

~ 14 ~
uncles and aunts | 1982
43

Contents   ~   ix

~ 15 ~
frankly, scarlett...
47

~ 16 ~
daily prayers | 2018
49

~ 17 ~
mediocrity | 2014
52

~ 18 ~
do as i say, not as i do | 2010
56

~ 19 ~
1986
59

~ 20 ~
myrtle neck, part two | 1980
69

~ 21 ~
biracial | 2019
73

~ 22 ~
myrtle neck, part three | 2020
77

~ 23 ~
he spoke it until it became truth | 2019
80

~ 24 ~
trust and believe | 2021
85

~ 25 ~
shattered/malibu nights | 2021
90

~ 26 ~
trust and believe, part two | 2022
97

~ 27 ~
coming to the table | 2020
102

~ 28 ~
soul crushing | 2020
106

~ 29 ~
a llamar al pan pan, y al vino vino
109

~ 30 ~
rebos is sober spelled backwards
114

~ 31 ~
i went to sleep | 2019
117

~ 32 ~
this ain't it | 2020
119

~ 33 ~

it's not you, it's me | 2021

121

~ 34 ~

moving goalposts | 2021

124

~ 35 ~

i don't want to know this much is true | 2022

129

~ 36 ~

i know this much is true | 2022

135

~ 37 ~

epilogue ~ home

138

~ 38 ~

vows to myself

141

~ 39 ~

acknowledgements

142

~ 40 ~

praise for i know this much is true

144

ABOUT THE AUTHOR - 146

LIMINAL

Her life, broken open

The writing's on the wall

She stops to take a breath

This step, it means everything

A world beyond her imagination

Her future in her own hands

~Ashley Castle Barnes, Liminal

~ 1 ~

SOMETHING BIGGER THAN YOURSELF

Yesterday I was clever, so I wanted to change the world.
Today I am wise, so I am changing myself.
~ Rumi

There are a plethora of inspirational quotes about becoming, dedicating yourself to, standing for, or being a part of *something bigger than yourself.* That's a beautiful thought, because we are all here to hold each other up and walk each other home. But how can you be something bigger than yourself if you don't first become your biggest self?

Marianne Williamson said in her book *A Return to Love* that we aren't really afraid of being inadequate, but rather we're afraid of recognizing our individual power. We don't like to come across as grandiose or braggart, so we shrink our talents into bite-sized pieces for our own and others' comfort. Playing small doesn't serve a higher purpose. Being degradingly humble doesn't add to the vibration of the universe. If we are constantly looking for our flaws, that's all we'll see. If we are constantly deprecating ourselves, we are bringing down the collective energy that creates change. When a baby is made, the egg or the sperm can't do anything by themselves. And an infertile egg can't be fertilized, nor can a dysfunctional swimming sperm reach the egg. Both parts must work at their highest function in order to create.

This isn't to say that we need to become conceited or narcissists. It just means that we need to do better at focusing on the things we are good at, and then reaching higher to improve. The best football players are doing drills, feeding their body well, and exercising almost daily to remain at top performance level. If we choose to stay stagnant and good enough, that's all we can expect to achieve in life.

Jesus tells us to love our neighbors, as we love *ourselves*; the husband is to love the wife, as he loves *himself*. In the 2014 commencement speech for Maharishi University, Jim Carrey said, "Like many of you, I was concerned about going into the world and doing something bigger than myself. Until someone smarter than me made me realize there is nothing bigger than myself".

Bigger than ourselves means part of the family, community, and humanity. If we want to see big changes occur in our families, communities, and humanity, we must start making the big changes in ourselves. There's the old saying that a chain is only as strong as its weakest link, and that applies in all aspects of life. If you want to see good in the world, the best place to start is with your own hands. If you want to see love in the world, the best place to start... is with yourself.

So I am starting with me.

MOMMA | 2020

The mother gives the child what she takes from herself.
~Friedrich Nietzsche

My mom and I sat on her front patio, as we often do when I visit. We talk about everything and nothing, and today was no different. I'm usually the one who asks questions about parenting, or our past family, and with each conversation we have, it seems I learn something new. How is it possible that I know so little about my own mother? And more so, how is it possible that I know so little about my own life growing up?

My mom is a very private person, apparently. She gets more open as we grow older, but still, I must be the one to prod. Maybe she doesn't know that I want to know *every little thing*. Maybe she herself doesn't remember things until I ask. Maybe I'm just way too nosey.

She drops the biggest bomb on me since, well, ever. I've just gotten my Ancestry DNA test results back and have found that I'm 1/3 black. Not American Indian like my father told us. Not 50% black like I suspected after researching his family tree. As usual, I'm left with more questions than answers when I try to learn about him. He is an enigma, a frustrating one at that, and I know so little about him.

My mom tells me that I was *two* before she married my father.

Internally, I combust.

"Does that mean that Anthony isn't my real father?" I ask, but I know the answer. Anthony is my real father. Her first husband, David was black as night, and my results from Ancestry would have shown a higher percentage if he was my father. I look too much like my half sister for anyone else to be my father. I act too much like my brother for anyone else to be my father. I know for a fact that David is not my father, but I ask it anyway.

Instead of my respect for my mother going down, she immediately becomes even more badass in my book. She comes across as this demure, quiet little mouse, and yet here she is, a once unwed mother. All this time, I was trying so hard to live up to the expectations I thought she had of me to be as proper as she, and she was just as human as the next person. My mom is the Mona Lisa. You just don't know what's hiding underneath.

And with this revelation, I realize that my mom hasn't judged me as much as I believed she did. I realize that my entire life, I have gaslit *myself*.

A WHOLE NEW LIFE | 2001

If you want to go quickly, go alone. If you want to go far, go together.
~African Proverb

Parenting is a series of constant course corrections. No two kids are alike, so there's no playbook. What works for one, absolutely does not work for another. I think I knew this innately, but it wasn't until my son was born, that I started to understand this. I had babysat my entire teen years, adored little kids, and was the self-proclaimed *Best Aunt Ever* to my niece. And then along came Raylan, this unique little boy unlike anyone I had ever encountered. I take that back; he was the clone of Calvin from Calvin & Hobbes.

Doug and I joked when I was pregnant that this kid would come out red-headed. Why, I don't know. But when he came out of the womb, cord wrapped around his neck, with a strip of red hair down the center of his head, I should have known what I was in for. The entire pregnancy was a hot mess, I was nauseated all waking hours, gained a metric ton of weight, and a whole host of other drama ensued with Doug's family. I had read so many articles, books, magazines, and had this idyllic dream of how everything would and should play out. Very little of it occurred. Raylan had issues latching from the beginning, but I was determined not to bottle feed my baby. We packed up our apartment in Georgia and moved to Tennessee when he was three days old. Once we got settled into our apartment in Tennessee, he decided sleep was not part of his game, and I was a sleep-deprived madwoman. Looking back, I'm sure there was some post-partum depression involved, but I refused to acknowledge or believe that I was capable of depression. It was a battle of wills...my precious, perfect, fussy baby, and my picture-perfect idea of what motherhood was going to be like, BY GOD.

Hillary Clinton once said that "it takes a village to raise a child". But I, got-dammit, did not need no stinkin' village to raise a child. And thus began the extreme self-gaslighting.

Growing up, I had been raised in a small, community-minded church. I have some of the best and worst memories from that environment. We associated with people of all ages, which provided depth to my interpersonal interactions. I was essentially the congregation babysitter, and every home that I went into, I was in awe of. I loved seeing how other mothers ran their households, the schedules, the organization, the food they consumed, even the folding of towels. I tucked away bits of information as notes on how I would one day be a wife and mother. Armed with all of this information, once I became a wife, I stepped into the role exceedingly well, especially for a 19-year-old. I assumed motherhood would be just as easy.

What I failed to realize was that the mothers I admired and hoped to emulate, had their own villages, and I as their babysitter, was part of that village. They could have date nights because of me. They could trust that their children were fed, bathed, read to, and played with, while they relaxed with their significant others. When they came back home, their children were asleep in bed, and other activities of the evening could commence. They also had other mothers, both older and their own ages, to commune with and learn from.

I had none of that.

Partly due to my stubbornness, and partly due to being newly relocated to an entirely unfamiliar state, I found myself alone all day with a constantly crying, always nursing, and never sleeping infant. My own mother was now 13 hours away, and my husband's family was an hour away and working full time. The picture-perfect household I envisioned was quickly fraying at the seams, but I would never admit it or ask for help. I could, and would, do it all.

New mothers are encouraged to nap when the baby naps, but since my baby didn't like to nap, that wasn't happening. Neither were the dishes, the laundry, or the dinners. Oh, the dinners! My new husband was an extremely picky eater, so I now had to learn how to cook new types of food: frozen chicken tenders, tater tots, hotdogs, sometimes meatloaf, biscuits and gravy. Vegetables, if any, had to be cooked to almost disintegration. This wasn't at all the way I had eaten growing up and through my adulthood, and the baby weight that was promised to come off from nursing, never did. I developed extreme social anxiety (on top of my already existing regular anxiety) and would sweat profusely whenever I had to go to the grocery store or anywhere for that matter, so the baby and I hardly ever went out.

Pulling from my memories, I decided that church was the best way to meet people, and maybe find some friends. I had grown up in a community church, the Kingdom Hall, and while I didn't fully ascribe to the entire belief system, I liked that it provided interactions with people of varying stages of life. There was a United Methodist church very close to our apartment, and I really liked the offerings they had, such as a Women's Bible Study, childcare, and a Men's Outreach. However, my husband, being raised Pentecostal, didn't want to attend there, so we looked for other churches. We found an Assembly of God church not too far from us and started attending. It was there that the self-gaslighting intensified even more.

EASTER SERVICE | 2003

I do not feel obliged to believe that the same God who has endowed us with sense, reason, and intellect has intended us to forgo their use.
~Galileo Galilei

Growing up, we had conventions twice a year. I always looked forward to the "dramas" that would break up the monotony of the all day long "Bible talks". Meetings and conventions were so silent, so proper, soooo utterly boring. Even the music could put you to sleep, and it was written in a key so high only an opera singer could do any justice to it.

It was Easter Sunday, and I knew we would of course hear about Jesus' crucifixion and resurrection. I'd heard the story hundreds of times already. I was grateful for his sacrifice, and whether he really was the son of God, or just a man who had very high convictions, he was someone to be admired.

Never in my life had I seen the story of Jesus depicted in such detail. The whips cracked over the speakers, and the man portraying Jesus cried out so believingly. I sobbed as they hung him up, and he told John to take care of his mother, Mary. My sins of my past suddenly burst forth to the surface, and I was so. very. unworthy. He loved me so much, that he died for me! So I could have access to his father! He loved me so much and wanted me to be in Heaven with him! How could I ever have thought to take this so lightly? How could I be so selfish to lie, cheat, steal, do drugs, have sex outside of marriage, drink? I vowed to be just like him, as much as I could, because he died for me. I would raise my children to be just like him, so they could live in heaven for eternity after they died. I would be the best wife, daughter, daughter in law and person, and lead by example for the rest of my days.

And when he walked out of the tomb, my breath caught in my chest, my heart stopped.

I believed.

~ 5 ~

HOLLIE HOBBIE | 1982

***The following chapter contains content involving childhood abuse/
sexual assault.***

*Be not ashamed, woman...
You are the gates of the body,
and you are the gates of the soul.
~Walt Whitman*

On my makeshift nightstand was a bottle of Wesson vegetable oil. My father was lying in my twin sized bed, in his boxers, atop the blanket my great-grandmother crocheted for me. It was bright and colorful, and he often stole it from my bed to use for himself. He would fall asleep smoking, and there were cigarette burns strewn all over the blanket. Him being in my bed was nothing new, he often worked nights, and slept in my room during the day. He had extreme back pain from his time in Korea, so sometimes he would sleep on the couch as well. I didn't particularly like him sleeping in

11

my bed, but I was raised not to question him, for fear we would be whipped with the belt.

I had been outside playing, as I often did, especially in the summer. We kids were basically expelled from the house so my father could sleep, and we knew to keep a distant perimeter from the house so he couldn't hear us yelling, screaming, laughing. If we were called inside, we knew we were in big trouble. So when I heard my name called through the window, my stomach tied in knots. I had been right outside my bedroom window when I was called, probably picking flowers, or hiding from the neighbor kids.

I reluctantly went inside the back door, through my parents' room, the kitchen, the living room, and into my room. I braced myself for the ensuing yelling and possible spanking I was used to.

Instead, my father told me to put on my nightgown. I was confused. But did as I was told. Maybe I was being sent to bed early instead of spanked. I would take that punishment *any* day, even though it was early afternoon. At least I could read, or go into my imagination. My father scooted over on the bed, and told me to get under the covers with him. He took off my underwear, poured some oil into his hands, and applied it to my private area. I was stunned. I knew what he was doing, I had seen it in his Penthouse magazines. But I couldn't move, or rebel. Next thing I knew, he was touching me in places I knew weren't supposed to be touched. He pushed my legs open wider, and I left my body, staring at the ceiling, waiting for him to leave me alone.

I don't remember how long it lasted, but I remember him telling me this was to stay between us. I remember when he was done, he told me to go take a shower and go back outside and play. I remember that it happened once more that summer, and that time, he had me touch him. I did, tentatively, but withdrew my hand in horror. He forced my hand on him again, and again, I pulled away. He got angry, shoved me away, and told me to go outside. I buried those memories far into my brain for years, but the father I thought I had, was now gone. I never looked at him the same again; everything he did and said after that summer was met with an undertone of hatred, disdain, and contempt. Whereas before, I felt sorry for his back pain, and night shift jobs, now I just thought he was an ass. I loved him and hated him all at once.

My grandmother wrote in her journals that she noticed a change in my personality that summer. I became sullen and angry, lashing out at her, misbehaving. I suddenly became aware of my clothes, making sure I covered up as much as I could. I quit playing with the boys in my neighborhood as much, while simultaneously wanting so desperately to run free with them as I had before. I wondered if now I was supposed to like them in a different way. Everything became so confusing. If I had made my own father want to be sexual with me, it was inevitable that the neighborhood boys would want that, too. My father began accusing me of being a slut, saying that the cold sores I would sometimes get were because I let too many boys kiss me. I hadn't even been kissed...I was TEN.

Before the summer ended, I burned the nightgown, and my favorite Hollie Hobbie halter top, the one I had been wearing the first time my father called me into the house. I would be 18 before I wore a two-piece bathing suit again.

~ 6 ~

LOT'S DAUGHTERS | 2019

This miserable fate
Suffer the wretched souls of those, who liv'd
Without or praise or blame, with that ill band
Of angels mix'd, who nor rebellious prov'd
Nor yet were true to God, but for themselves
Were only. From his bounds Heaven drove them forth,
Not to impair his lustre, nor the depth
Of Hell receives them, lest th' accursed tribe
Should glory thence with exultation vain.
~Dante's Inferno
Canto 3

John F. Kennedy, although well-red, misquoted via paraphrase Dante's *Inferno*, saying, "The hottest places in hell are reserved for those who, in times of great moral crisis, maintain their neutrality." The point still stands: there are some things you must be either for or against, there is no middle ground.

It was another Sunday morning at church, October 2019. I loved church, no I adored church. I loved the music, I loved our pastor,

14

I loved learning about God's love for me. I loved that my kids (usually) loved church, and that they had made some good friends there. Even though Doug and I hadn't really ventured much into finding our own friends, church on Sunday morning was still my happy place. When the kids were little, it was the one time I was able to take for myself to dress up and feel pretty. As they got older, it was the one time where I felt we were somewhat actually a family.

This sermon started off as usual. I took notes on my phone because it helped me pay attention, and I always thought that one day...ONE DAY when I got my shit together, I would refer to those notes, and do what I don't know. But like everything in my life, I saved things for that one day when I would have time to reflect and savor. (I've since lost all the notes on my phone...some 300 of them...) Our pastor always had something good and meaty to speak on, and today was no different. I was rapt with attention. Church here was so different than the congregation in which I grew up; it was interesting, and lively, and I felt the topics spoken on made sense in a real-life way.

Since I've lost all my notes, I can't recall how the story of Lot in Genesis 19 was related, and having heard the story many times before, I went along with the sermon. Until I heard,

"But before they lay down, the men of the city, the men of Sodom, both young and old, all the people to the last man, surrounded the house; and they called to Lot, "Where are the men who came to you tonight? Bring them out to us, so that we may know them." Lot went out of the door to the men, shut the door after him, and said, "I beg you, my brothers, do not act so wickedly. Look, I have two daughters who have not known a man; let me bring them out to you, and do to them as you please; only do nothing to these men, for they have come under the shelter of my roof."

My daughter was now 15 years old.

I stopped typing my notes.

This. Was. Unacceptable.

I went home and read the chapter before, and the chapter after. I read about Dinah in Genesis 34. THIS is what I had been ascribing to for all these years? It was if suddenly a light switch was flipped on, a bright, glaring light, and I had been in absolute darkness before.

PATRIARCHY.

I'll ascribe to patriarchy all damn day long if I have to. It's what I know. It's familiar. It's easy. It's in our DNA as women. But you will not force my daughter to sign up for that. I will not allow my daughter to be taught from a place of reverence that she is a commodity to be traded, that her worth is connected to what is between her legs, that her value is sum zero, that she can be offered up to men to keep them quiet and appeased. And though the church we attended did their best to put women in positions of leadership, it wasn't enough. There was still too much talk about purity culture, and the responsibility for upholding it geared toward girls more than guys; still too much talk about husbandly headship; still too much talk about not usurping the hierarchy. Put your boot on my neck, fine; put your boot anywhere near my daughter, and I'll burn this whole damn place to the ground.

~ 7 ~

COME AS YOU ARE | 2009

Don't be mean. We don't have to be mean. Cause, remember, no matter
where you go, there you are.
~Buckaroo Banzai

Nirvana's angst-ridden, heavy basslined music has always resonated so deeply with me, even when I don't always understand the meaning behind Kurt's lyrics. Just the feeling of being an outspoken outcast made me feel like I could have written the music myself.

I've never fit in with the crowd. Never been a leader or a follower. I've just blazed my way through life, burning my own path, and usually setting fire to most everything I touch. For almost 30 years this worked for me, until I moved to the south and joined a southern family.

I'm an enneagram 8, and a female on top of that. It's great if you're a male 8; but female 8's are often called a bitch, plain and simple. I don't have flowy language, I'm blunt, I listen to hip hop & Nirvana & Alice In Chains, I cuss, I wish I could wear converse all the time, and I couldn't care less to burn a bridge with you. When I'm done, I'm done. I sometimes watch the NBA, and can hang a

17

shelf. I abhor frivolous conversation. But I'm also the friend you call if you need help burying the body. And I will stick up for you every single time someone wrongs you.

This new family had had no idea how to react to the brazen Floridian who had just entered their family like a Hurricane. I'd only known their son/brother for 3 months and we were already getting married!? Of course they were wary. Immediately I became the source of contention and the target of their fearful attacks.

I had just stepped out of a time in my life that was full of drama and poor choices. At first, I was floored that I wasn't immediately liked, as previously, anyone I encountered either absolutely adored or simply tolerated me for who I was. These two things combined, along with my new husband's extreme anti-confrontational nature, I internalized their images of me and figured I must be an asshole and I needed to change completely.

I shrunk myself, participating less and less in real life conversations. I tried to forge myself into this uber-Christian woman, and be quieter, use smaller vocabulary, read less (because whenever I learn something new, I have to tell everyone about it and obviously no one wanted to hear what I had to say, I was a YANKEE, God forbid!), and just not have an opinion about anything. It pacified the new family for a time, but I became a doormat. Allowing things to be done and said that no normal person would permit, I kept my mouth shut, biding my time until this tribulation would end. On the rare occasions I would speak up, sticking up for my kids or my husband or my mother-in-law, I was immediately shut down and set in my place.

I allowed it to happen because I thought I deserved it. I thought I deserved to be punished for all the wrongs I had committed in my past, and who was I to question how God choose to dole that punishment out? God uses everyone for everything, so I just assumed He was using my new family to inflict His wrath that I felt I so deserved.

WRONG.

I sit here today and realize how WRONG I was. I was being so arrogant in my intended humbleness. God, the Universe, Great Spirit, whatever, don't require us to be contorted doormats in order to prove a point or gain favor. It's spitting in the face of the Universe to assume that we aren't good enough, and allow other flawed humans who can barely acknowledge their own essence to dictate how to exude ours. We permit others who don't know how to live their own vivaciousness to judge and break the spirit that was innately gifted to us.

~ 8 ~

MYRTLE NECK, PART ONE | 1976

When life gives you lemons, fuck the lemons and bail.
~Mike Thompson

I sat on my grandparent's bed, chatting excitedly with them. We tried to come up with names for my new baby brother or sister. I just knew it was going to be a brother, even though I really wanted a sister. I wanted a captive audience and permanent best friend for the rest of my life. I wanted someone to dress up like my dollies, and play tea party with. A brother would provide none of that. All the books I had read up to this ripe old age of four years and four months had indicated that sisters were sisters for life, and brothers were nothing but a nuisance.

When I first saw Michael, I was instantly in love. Brother or not, he was mine. He looked like an alien, with brown wrinkled skin, a weirdly shaped head, and a forehead like an old man's. He was tiny, and yet, looked wise beyond his years. I loved looking at his fingers and toes, and secretly wished his legs were fat and chunky because I thought that's what babies were supposed to look like.

It never occurred to me that I would lose time with my mom, who at this point in my life was both my best friend and my subordinate. I'm sure by this point, I was already bossy, demanding "wopples" (waffles) and Captain Kangaroo. My mom says I was "born grown", and has occasionally deemed me the moniker "The Little General". But lose time with my mom I did, and I retaliated my anger at not being the center of her attention by stealing my brother's diapers and peeing in them in my closet. Part of that was rebellion at being four years and four months and no longer having my mom's attention, because I obviously did not want to be a baby; and part of it was sheer curiosity at how diapers actually worked. I've always been fascinated with the how and why of the most ridiculous things.

I adored this new addition to our family, even though he was the biggest pain in the butt ever, as brothers are supposed to be. Being the youngest, he seemed to get away with a lot more than I did, and I was both jealous and in love. He grew to have a mass of curls atop his head, as I did when I was his age, but being a boy, everyone seemed to focus on his rather than mine. By now, my hair was almost black, straight and down to my waist. By the time he was two, and I was six, my grandmother took me to her salon and had my hair chopped off. I wanted it in a wedge, like Dorothy Hamill, it ended up just looking like a boy.

Mikey Mikey Mikey. Everyone loved Mikey. He was charismatic from birth, it seemed, and I wanted to be just like him. I was starting to see cracks in my parents' marriage here and there, not enough to be alarmed yet, but my father wasn't perfect anymore. I knew that I could rely on him for the most part, especially for the truth, but the façade was slipping. So my brother became my new idol.

I loved seeing him sitting on the steps outside our apartment when I came home from school, waiting for me. I felt special. I loved coming home from visiting my grandparents and him being so excited to see me, too. One particular trip, however, I came home to see that he had drawn all over the face of one of my favorite dolls. I had left it in my room, on the bed, and yet I was chastised for not putting it away. I felt I was too young to have to be this responsible, and was more angry at my mom than my brother. This became a pattern in my life, blaming my mom for too many things.

We moved to Florida when I was eight, and Mikey was four. I flew down ahead, and my mom, brother and Auntie Gail drove the U-Haul. I've always been secretly jealous that he got to have that road trip with my mom, but I'm sure I would have been a nightmare. There was never enough entertainment, and if I was bored, I would talk. Incessantly. My grandmother would bribe me with snacks and little coloring books on our drives to and from Florida just so I would shut up. I'm sure she was the one who invented "Quiet Time" just to get some peace from my ever-running mouth. I have cassette tapes that we used to send back and forth to each other since long distance phone calls cost per minute, and who wanted to spend $300 million listening to me prattle on? The tapes are 60 minutes each side, and I barely give anyone else a minute to talk themselves. I read stories, and tell stories, and just. Talk. So. Much.

When my brother and I are together again in Florida, we move in with Gramma and Grampa until we can find a house to rent. My brother and I run all over their back yard, playing hide and seek in the trees, playing in the sandbox, and at night, running around and around their floor fan. He earns the nickname "Two Moons" because as he runs, his diaper slips lower and lower, until his hind end is hanging out. I think he adores me, too, and does whatever I tell him. We mimic the noise of my mom's hairdryer, and make noises into the fan, distorting our voices. Even though I had originally wanted a sister, I decide that a brother is way better. Boy games are so much more fun, and dangerous, and exciting. They play with trucks, and throw rocks, and climb trees. They are loud and rambunctious, and hardly anyone reprimands them for it. Girls are supposed to be quiet and ladylike, and I hate it.

$$\sim 9 \sim$$

DEMEROL | 2005

Waking up when the pain is too intense, then passing out between contractions

Yelling this is so stupid why would anyone do this

    fuck this

Glimpses of peeking through closed eyes then shutting them again, thinking no it's not time to wake up yet
    it's too early

Then suddenly someone wakes you up with smelling salts

    Violently

        Abruptly

You awaken from the dream, and can never go back to the same
dream again

You try to go back to sleep, but have lost your place in the dream

You can't go back to sleep, now you must shake it off

                                                    And you ask

Was it real? Or was it a dream?

Even though you chose to take this nap,
                    you still wake up in a fog,
                                    with a headache

Even though you chose to take this nap,
                                    you still wish you hadn't slept
so long

~ 10 ~

CRY IT OUT, PART ONE | 2018

Our virtues and our failings are inseparable, like force and matter.
When they separate, man is no more.
~Nikola Tesla

I sat on the floor outside his bedroom door, tears streaming down my face. He was 15 months old, and we were finally going the cry it out route. We had been living in an apartment previously, so I did everything I could to make sure we didn't wake the neighbors with his every two hours waking and wailing. But now that we had bought a house, it was time for me to get a full night's sleep, especially with the new baby coming in January.

It took 4 nights, and he finally slept. It was the most heart wrenching sound ever, hearing the baby that you dreamt of for your whole life, wailing for you to hold him to sleep.

A month later, we moved, and he didn't sleep through the night again until he went to kindergarten.

And here I sit, 16 years later, tears streaming down my face, anticipating him crying himself to sleep. Thinking we abandoned him. Thinking we hate him. Thinking he hates us.

When he was 15 months old, he forgot those feelings by the time he got older, or so the cry it out experts say. He's not going to forget this so easily. He's not going to forgive this so easily, especially when the reasons he's going aren't so black and white. He's not a door-slammer like I was. He doesn't yell at us or call us names. For the most part, he does what he's supposed to...when he wants and deems necessary. He has a job, and they love him. Adults are always so impressed with how well-spoken he is.

Being a self-proclaimed Hippie Mom, I thought it was important to give my kids a voice. To let them speak their mind and always feel like they were important, and their opinion held value. I never felt that way growing up (no offense, Ma), and I wanted to do things differently. I thought I was doing things better. I tried to parent with grace, looking at their actions and mistakes like I thought God looked at mine. How could I ask a child to do something the first time I asked, when I knew full well that as an adult, I didn't do a lot of things that God asked? I wanted so badly to be like Jesus, full of forgiveness and understanding. Go and sin no more, seventy times seven, and all that.

But the thing that is supposed to go hand in hand with God's Grace is that we are supposed to be grateful for that grace, and make the choice to try and abide by the boundaries He set forth for us. Grace and forgiveness isn't a once saved/always saved deal, where you are covered regardless of what you do, and thus you can do whatever you want. Grace and forgiveness is a gift, and an opportunity to do better.

I'm not sure children really understand that the same way adults do. I was parenting from an adult point of view, from my end of the street, thinking that if I forgave and overlooked and made excuses, that one day, it would all be appreciated, and it would click.

19 months until graduation, and it still hasn't clicked. I'm not expecting him to have his whole life planned out by now, or be a straight A student, or star athlete, but I do expect him to be an example to his sister, respectful to others who are unlike him, have

a love for God, and try to live up to the potential that I know he holds within. There's no glimmer of even one of those things, nothing I can really grasp onto in hopes that one day soon it'll click. 19 months left to try and make sure my child doesn't end up homeless, or an addict, or on a slab, or regretting not trying.

That's the biggest thing. What will I regret more: him being angry at me for what could be a very long time but a higher chance he'll be the amazing person I know him to be; or letting him stay on this path that is 100% unknown where he will end up?

So I'll let him cry it out, hoping that someday soon, we will all sleep better.

Sitting outside this door is the second most heart wrenching thing, ever.

~ 11 ~

THERE WAS A TIME YOU WOULDN'T HAVE PUT UP WITH THIS SHIT | 2019

If love does not know how to give and take
without restrictions,
it is not love,
but a transaction that never fails to lay stress on a plus and a
minus.
~Emma Goldman

I thought, growing up, that my mom was weak for staying with my father. Then as I grew older, I saw that she really was strong. It takes a lot of strength and courage to stay with someone who beats you down constantly, and still get up and do what needs to be every day. So when I found myself in a similar situation, I emulated my mom because I thought it was right for the kids.

But then I realized that I was actually playing into a game that I didn't fully believe in, and definitely didn't want my daughter to play. I was demonstrating weakness and complacency for her. All three of us, my mom, myself and my daughter. Was I going to leave the burden of breaking the cycle on my daughter's shoulders?

I assumed that I was supposed to be a martyr in order to be a good mother. I thought that I was supposed to give up everything that I wanted in order for my children to have a good life.

But when my Dad, and then my mom, told me I was a grown, smart, strong, capable woman, I saw that my daughter needed me to step forward. My mom needed me to step forward. She's been waiting on me. I don't know her reasons for why she was too afraid to do it, but I see now that she's been waiting for me.

My mom and I had a pretty strained, on and off relationship for years. I felt deserted, betrayed, and neglected after the incident with my father. We didn't trust each other through my high school years, and for a few years after I graduated. Her hope was that I conformed to the religion to which she ascribed, and I just couldn't go along with their beliefs. I sometimes wonder if I had been completely honest with her and explained why I didn't believe as they did, if that would have garnered her respect on some level. That's the thing about religious extremism: you feel that you can't voice your dissent, because you get a canned response in return; and when someone leaves the "flock", it's viewed as a failure on the part of the parents first, then the church. It's really just that we have free will, different thoughts and ideas. And yeah, free will. Religion is a system of control.

When my son was born and I was thrown into a whole new system of life, new family, new husband, new baby, new state, new almost everything, I started calling my mom regularly. Many of those calls were in a fury, or in tears. This was one time I couldn't figure things out on my own. Was it me? Was it the baby? Was it the in-laws? Was it the ex-wife? What was the problem? I had no answers, and neither did she. But she listened, and that helped tremendously. She did research on strong-willed children, and ADHD. She consoled me as best she could. As strained as our relationship had been, I'm sure it was hard for her to hear her 30-year-old daughter, incoherently sobbing. "I can't do this, Mom. I don't know what I'm doing wrong. I don't know how to fix this. I don't know what to do".

There were times I wanted to end it all. I was exhausted. I was frustrated. This wasn't what I had envisioned for my life, ever, and definitely not when I had gotten married. I could see no end in sight. But I didn't want to die, I wanted to see this through to the end. I've always believed things will always get better if I just hold on a little longer. Suicide is a permanent solution to a temporary problem, I would recite over and over again. I had a niece that I adored, and wanted to watch grow up. I had this tiny little baby boy that I just knew was given to me as a gift. And then, when he was just 11 months old, I found out I had another on the way.

Message boards were my lifeline to the outside world. Raylan was a very unsatisfied baby, so any outing ended early due to a meltdown on either his or my part. I would sweat profusely at the grocery store, just feeling others' eyes boring into the back of my head because my kid was screaming his face off in the store. When I wasn't calling my mom in tears, I was posting on message boards, subtly begging for answers while not trying to sound like the lunatic I felt I was becoming. I will forever be grateful to the women on these boards who supported me in their own ways, giving me tidbits of information that would lead me to research all avenues of possibilities. Because of them, by the time I ended my marriage, I knew that I had exhausted every single option.

"I would have stayed with you forever. I would have turned myself inside out for you." ~Birdee Pruitt, *Hope Floats*

The suggestions I received from these women on the boards ranged from "If it were me, I would take his video games and smash them in the driveway", to "Pray more, try this book, The Power of the Praying Wife". As much as I wanted to, and as angry as I was with how my marriage was, there was no way I could bring myself to smash his video games, set his clothes on fire, or pack my things and just leave. Having two little ones, it just wasn't an option for me. I had met this man with the goal to do better, be a better person, and I knew the universe had my back. If things weren't working out, it was my fault, there was something I just had to be overlooking.

I joined a Christian message board, and the women there were all happy and successful in their marriages. Perfect. I have people I can now emulate without resorting to violence. I chatted with them all day, every day, between caring for my kids and reading *all* the Christian books. I had torn through the entire Left Behind series when my father-in-law loaned them to me. I had hoped that reading the books would give us something to bond over, and maybe through that, they would finally see me and the good qualities I had. My father-in-law, especially, loved to comment on my weight, my parenting, the way I spoke, and where I was from. Assuming that all people are good and decent at their core, I worked fervently to get this family to *just freaking like me*; and even though my husband said they did, the things that came out of their mouth seemed to show otherwise.

Reading the many, many Christian books further cemented how horrible, awful a person I was. The only hope for anything getting better was Heaven, and all that we could do meanwhile was rejoice in our suffering and pray. Jesus Fucking Christ, I prayed. Upon waking, "God please help me to be a good mom, and a good wife. Help me to ignore those who want to start problems, and glue my damn mouth shut" (maybe I shouldn't have said "damn", maybe that's why my prayers weren't answered). Throughout the day, "God please help me to just be patient, forgiving and loving. Help me to show my husband and kids and family the way You love. Let me reflect You in all things". At night, "I'm so sorry, God, that I didn't do better today. Please forgive me. Please give me another chance tomorrow. I promise I'll talk to you more through the day, because obviously I am a terrible person and can't do this without you constantly by my side. Please wash me clean of all the things I do and say and think." All day long, I berated myself for every little mishap. I was sure I was constantly being punished. I second-guessed *every single thing* I thought, did, said, or didn't do. I was relentless in shaming myself.

All I wanted was for Jesus to come back so I could just breathe and rest. Even then, I wasn't sure I would even get to go to Heaven, because I was incessantly screwing up. It was as if I was outside myself most of the time, watching every move I made, every word I said, every thought I had, and screaming at myself what a shitty person, wife and mom I was. If I could, I would have just moved into church so I could just park myself at the altar of forgiveness, because apparently I wasn't asking for it enough. I couldn't catch a break from myself, or from the outside influences who kept knocking at our door wanting to come in and cause drama. I begged my husband to just close the door, stop answering his ex's every single call; or let me hide in another room with my own door locked, and not make me have to go visit his family. But he had a reason for everything.

Logic Magic.

Knowing what your own personal boundaries are is not a bad thing; expecting others to understand them can be unrealistic. Yet, that's what individual boundaries are for: our own personal use. We don't have to explain or make others understand or conform to our boundaries. We are allowed to not date people who don't fit into our vision of our own lives, regardless of the time we've been with them. Regardless of whether we've kissed them, slept with them, are engaged to them, married to them, or have kids with them.

Personal relationship choices are personal. You have boundaries of your choosing. A relationship should make both people happy, and changing your boundaries just to make someone else happy, comfortable, or because they have a different opinion than yours will probably not make you happy...or honest.

We all have our own personal, specific needs, wants and standards. Does this make us wrong? No, we are not wrong for knowing our limits. What is wrong, is expecting others to meet those limits when they've shown their inability to do so; or diminishing our own standards to meet theirs just to keep the relationship together. This is dishonesty to them, and ourselves.

Women do not owe their affection, sex or relationship energy to anyone. We get to choose who we invest that energy into. We can choose to set boundaries with someone who doesn't pull the weight we request. We can choose the things we look for in a potential partner, and the things that will increase or decrease the attraction we hold for a person. Relationships are a two-way street, and are created to serve and benefit both people involved. When two people enter into a relationship, the onus shouldn't fall on one person to dispose of their standards. Everyone has different standards and ideas about what works in a relationship, and whatever that criteria needs to be for you is nobody's business or choice but yours.

What we choose to do as a society can be a completely different issue than what we choose to do as an individual. We can love and hold grace for society, but that doesn't mean we are required to engage with those we love and hold grace for on a one to one basis. You can have compassion and not judge others for why they are the way they are, for how they interact within a relationship, and still choose not to be involved with that person.

We are all within our own personal rights and freedoms to state boundaries regarding what we can and cannot deal with. It doesn't make us wrong, selfish, not a good or bigger person. Everyone is deserving of love, but we also must be real with ourselves about what we can cope with financially, physically, mentally, and emotionally.

My opinions, needs, wants, and desires for what I expected out of a relationship were, and still are not, wrong. They were simply different than Doug's. And the same goes for his opinions, needs, wants and desires for what he expected out of a relationship. Had we dated longer, we would have either discovered this and moved on, or we would have found a compromise. Being thrown in head first into marriage and parenthood so early on didn't allow for that natural progression.

You should not have to break yourself into bite sized pieces to be more palatable for someone else. You should not have to contort yourself into boxes in which you are not meant to fit. You should not have to walk paths that are not yours to follow.

There are few things more personal than what a person looks for and will tolerate in a partner. Yet, there is no end to what people will take offense to, and, in their hurt and insecurity, turn their innermost frustrations outward towards the alleged offender. We will resort to calling people selfish, or a narcissist, when our needs aren't being met. We will villainize the other, because we feel stuck, trapped, in a situation that, quite frankly, we permitted to occur. Because we chose not to be honest with ourselves. Because we chose to allow another person's opinions and values color our own. Because we were feeling guilty for past offenses that we believed another person knew a better way for us than we knew for ourselves. We heard the names we were called, the insults directed towards us just because we had different ideals, and allowed them to momentarily question our own reality.

Rather than shutting the door on past transgressions and resting in faith that forgiveness was granted, we chose to wear the cloak of shame bestowed upon us by another, far-removed judge of our character. We didn't believe that forgiveness from the harmed party was enough. We didn't believe that forgiveness from a higher power was enough. We sat in the court of another human being, one who was completely unaware of our essence, and deemed them worthy of omniscience.

And truly, there was a time when you wouldn't have put up with that shit.

~ 12 ~

CRY IT OUT, PART TWO | 2022

*Sometimes, only one person is missing, and the whole world seems
depopulated.*
~Alphonse de Lamartine

"Look what I made Ethan, Mom." My daughter had made a
montage video for her boyfriend on their one year anniversary. It
was set to the song, "You!" by LANY. I watched the video showing
them, during the course of their relationship, dancing in the rain,
laughing, wrestling, making TikTok videos, and snuggling, and my
heart caught in my chest, tears welling in my eyes. She looked at
me queerly, "Are you crying?" I said, "I love that you have someone
you feel that way about." and quickly checked my emotions.

It had been years since I had felt that way about someone. I'd
hoped to keep that feeling I once had about their dad for years to
come, but amidst all the drama and life circumstances, the feeling
faded.

It was part of the reason why I had become so enamored with
church: singing what were basically love songs to Jesus. Feeling
deep, raw emotions for someone, anyone. Certainly I felt strong

emotions for my kids...I was madly in love with them. I was one of the few moms who relished the end of school so that I could have them all to myself for the summer, and crushed when school would begin again. Not to say that there weren't days I wanted to offer them on a buy one, get one free special, but the majority of my days at home, I adored and cherished every minute I had with these fascinating creatures. Everything they did and do is filled with wonderment for me: their singing, their dancing, their growth, their sports...

Their very fucking existence. Just the fact that they happened in my life at the exact time they did never ceases to amaze me. I am the luckiest person alive.

I waited as long as I possibly could to leave their dad, and when I finally did, they came around often enough to stave off the sadness I felt when they weren't there. Oddly enough, it seems as if I saw them more often when I was homeless and living in my office, sleeping on my massage tables, and showering at the rec center. When I finally got an apartment of my own, I expected the visits to continue.

I wait to greet them on the front steps as they get off the bus. I sit expectantly in car pool line to pick them up. I willingly drive them anywhere they ask. I linger at bedtime until they drift off to sleep. No matter how exhausted I am, if they wake me up in the middle of the night, I give one more hug or answer their text. Just knowing they are under the same roof as me is enough. Just being in their presence fills my cup. I want to spend every moment I can with them, because I know, one day all too soon, they'll have lives of their own. I'm somewhat secure in the fact that they know I will always be there should they need me, but less secure in knowing whether they will want me.

When I had COVID in February 2022, by the end of the week, my heart was desperate to see them. I got to their house and grabbed tightly, smelling their hair and soaking their essence. Five minutes is enough, but at the same time, it's so precious little.

I drive back to my apartment, like a junkie who has gotten their fix, and it wears off less than a mile down the road. My heart tightens again, and my breath catches. Here come the tears. I know full well I'll be seeing them again tomorrow, but they're not *with* me. I can't knock on their door and just say "Hi, I love you." I'm not right there if they can't sleep. I can't lay on their bed and watch them play video games or scroll on their phone.

What mother in their right mind would leave their kids behind? Am I so selfish that I prioritized myself over them? Couldn't I have waited until they moved out to leave? No, I couldn't. Staying even one more year, I would have completely lost myself. I was barely there to grasp as it was, had more time gone by and I would have slipped so far deep under the murky waters, air gone from my lungs.

So I sit, once more in my life, and this time it's me who cries it out.

~ 13 ~

A GOLDEN CHORD | 2020

I used to think I was the strangest person in the world but then I thought there are so many people in the world, there must be someone just like me who feels bizarre and flawed in the same ways I do. I would imagine
her, and imagine that she must be out there thinking of me, too. Well, I hope that if you are out there and read this and know that, yes, it's true I'm here, and I'm just as strange as you.
~ Frida Kahlo

I've carried around this thought for over 20 years...A Golden Chord. I read the words in passing in a book, and it struck me, as things sometime do, and stuck with me for all these years. Like a seedling kept in a greenhouse, I've kind of just let it slowly germinate, and I think now it's finally time to let it unfurl.

All my life I've wrestled with my belief system. Guilt was something that was so deeply imprinted in my very soul, that any time I deviated from anything that was remotely UN-Christian, I panicked. Any time I fell short, I immediately felt overwhelming guilt that I was disappointing or bringing shame to my family, and fearing the ensuing banishment that would soon follow. Hearing my grand-mother's "for shame!" or my mother saying my name in that drawn out, disappointed tone sent me churning into turmoil. Any time something went "wrong", my default was to look internally at what sin I may have committed to bring this on; and unfortunately, that type of thinking spread into my views of other people. Someone's child would get sick? Hmmm, I wonder what they must have done. Someone having financial problems? Oh, that's because you don't go to church. How sickening.

When you place this thinking on others, you are constantly turning it back on yourself as well, even if you aren't blatant about it. It can show up later, in the form of undiagnosed autoimmune issues, or depression, or chronic fatigue.

Why?

A Golden Chord.

We're beings of energy, and like bees pollinating flowers with the pollen from another plant, our energy rubs off on other people. That energy originates from a divine source...you might call it Collective Conscious, others call it the Universe, I call it Divine God. That source is infinite, effervescent, golden light, transmitted into each of us through that Golden Chord. Why Chord and not Cord?

Webster defines it as such:

Chord /kôrd/ : a group of (typically three or more) notes sounded together, as a basis of harmony

If you've read the Bible, there's a scripture that says a cord of 3 strands is not easily broken (Ecclesiastes 4:12), and where two or more are gathered, I am with them (Matthew 18:20). When we are aligned with those around us, in community, it's a beautiful thing...harmonious, strong, and actually OF God/Universe/Divine.

Think of it like this: We are each like the iOS hard drive on an iPhone. At the core, we're all the same beautiful beings of light. All made in the same image. But then, we each download our own individual apps. That's what makes us unique. Mine might have more music on it, yours might have more educational apps, someone else might have more games on theirs. Sometimes we password protect them to keep them safe. Sometimes, though... we share things to the cloud. Sharing to the cloud makes certain things on our phones accessible to others. Those are the thoughts and information that we put out there for all to see, and sometimes upload for themselves. We're pollinating.

Am I pollinating with grace and compassion? Or am I pollinating with contempt and judgement? It's time to clean out some of my apps... the ones loaded with guilt and frustration and discord. For so long, I've felt like not enough a Christian because I don't read my Bible every day or sometimes when I sit in church, I question what's being said. Sometimes I drop the F bomb, and sometimes I drink. *I'm not being a good sheep.*

I've never felt so phony as I do when I sit with a group of Christians who walk their walk.

I've never felt so ME as I do when I journal and write to God; or when I run and see sunsets from my creator.

The guilt is so consuming. So all encompassing. And at the same time, I feel like this is right.

When I stopped going to church, I was surprised that I didn't feel the pang of guilt as I expected I would. It's not that I no longer believe in God, I just don't believe in the bastardized version that some sects of religion have done to the essence of who Jesus was. We're taught that in order to be worthy of love, we need to wear this heavy parka of guilt, always scrutinizing our every move and thought. We're taught that today, here and now, isn't important, and we're always supposed to have our eyes and heart set on this distant promise of heaven. Heaven can be here, on earth, right now. We fear making mistakes because of the threat of hell. Humans believe that they are the most advanced species on earth, but at the same time, we don't have trust that we can be intrinsically good. If I don't call myself a Christian, it won't be because I worship the devil. My tribe is not in the traditional Christian church. My tribe is made up of people who love me for me, who push me to be better without making me feel less than, and who know my heart fully. God is beautifully infused in all of us, and we can't escape it.

~ 14 ~

UNCLES AND AUNTS | 1982

Sometimes people don't want to hear the truth because they don't want their illusions destroyed.
~ Friedrich Nietzsche

Growing up, my father had lots of people in and out of our house, usually men. My brother and I called them our "uncles". Uncle David, Uncle Shank, Uncle Tony, are the ones I can recall off-hand. I think it was my father's way of putting a title of respect on them from a child's point of view, and I think he was attempting to create a brotherhood or community for himself. His family was all deceased, except for his sister, Cleo, and my mom had no siblings herself.

Uncle David owned a shop of some sort, but what I do remember were the candy sticks he sold in jars. They were colorful, with a white stripe that wrapped around them. I'm pretty sure he sold them for a nickel apiece, but I was allowed to pick one each time we visited him. He was always very nice to me, and I loved tagging along with my father to visit him, because we would always pass the "Sleeping Giant" on the drive to West Hartford.

43

Uncle Shank was a big, black man, with a salt and pepper beard. I don't know why I loved him, but he seemed like a big teddy bear to me. He would come to our apartment occasionally to visit, which was rare for us to have visitors other than the neighbors. I remember my father yelling at my mom after his visits, accusing her of cheating on him with Uncle Shank. It never made sense to me, because Uncle Shank was my father's friend first.

Uncle Tony was Tony and Joe's father, the boys who lived across the street from us in our rental in Florida. They lived in a big white, wooden house, different from all the other houses on that street, which were made of cinderblock. I never went inside their house until after they moved out, and it was falling apart. I would get yelled at for getting caught going in there, so I always made sure to explore it when my father was at work. Uncle Tony was SO COOL. He was Polynesian-bred, so he was short and small boned. Tan, with long black hair, always smiling and joking. He seemed like such a fun father, and I often wished mine would go away so I could have a new one. His wife, Amy, was blonde and gorgeous. She would lay in their yard, slather herself with baby oil, and declare "Ok Mr. Sun, do your stuff!" They seemed like such a sexy couple, like the ones you would see on late-night TV, and so unlike my own parents.

Then there was another uncle, whose name escapes me. He was handsome, and much younger than my parents, maybe late twenties. He was tan, brown-haired, and good-looking. He lived with us for a short time, and would give us change to walk up to the convenience store for sodas. He seemed no different than any of our other "uncles", so there was no need for me to have my guard up, even though he lived with us at the end of the summer I was ten. He was a distraction for my father, so we got yelled at a lot less, and I had already buried what my father had done to me by then. My mom had decided to put me in summer camp a couple weeks after it happened. Even though she had no idea what was going on, I was grateful for the break away from my father during the day. I would wander around Shore Acres Rec Department grounds, listening to the music they played from the loudspeakers. Climaxx Blues Band's song "I Love You", and Foreigner's "Waiting for a Girl Like You" seemed to be on repeat that summer, but they were a reprieve for me.

One day, my father told us the uncle was moving out. We were sad to see him go, but we'd had so many people come and go through our lives already that it was no big deal. He put his bags in his red truck, and started off down the street. I ran behind the truck, yelling goodbye, when he stopped at the end of the street. Naively, I thought he had a present for me. I ran up to the truck, he rolled down the window and said "Give me a hug goodbye!" I reached through the window to hug him, and he stuck his tongue in my mouth.

I repeat, I was TEN.

Not long after, a woman moved in with us. She seemed so wise, and talked to me like I was an actual person. She taught me how to do backbends, back walkovers, and we were just getting down my back handspring when my father threw her out.

My father told us he was American Indian, and we believed him. We would go to schools around Florida dressed in regalia, and my father would give educational talks to the students on American Indian life. Then my brother, Tony, Joe and I would perform some dances while my father drummed. This woman went along with us. Then my father got the call he wanted so badly, from the St. Petersburg Pier. They had permitted him to do a performance at the Pier. He was so excited. I was not. I was tired of missing school, of being forced to wear regalia, and performing the same dance over again. During the summer, the woman made being an Indian interesting. She showed me her beadwork, and made fires in our yard, which I loved. I'm a closet pyromaniac.

We loaded up the car and van and drove to the Pier. We set up the stage. We did our performance. My father got angry with me because I wasn't performing to his liking, but it was hot. The regalia was thick and heavy. Afterwards, we began packing up, and wanting to get away from my father, I followed the woman to her car, hoping she would offer to take me home instead of having to ride with my father and the boys. We were three feet from her car, when I heard my father whistle for me, then yelling loudly to get my ass back to him. I ignored him. He came running. He grabbed me by the arm roughly, and then started yelling at the woman, and me, accusing her of trying to kidnap me. I was confused. Was she really trying to kidnap me? Was I really this stupid, again?

She defended herself, saying she was only going to bring me home. That I didn't need to ride with smelly, sweaty boys. I looked back and forth between them as they yelled at each other, very loudly. My father told her to pack her shit and get out of his house before he got home. He yanked me by the arm up the sidewalk to the van, cussing at me the entire way. "You should fucking know better than to go off with fucking strangers! Are you fucking stupid? She wants to rape and kill you! She's a fucking drug addict and a whore! You're God damn lucky I came after you, or you would be fucking cut up just like Adam Walsh and we would never fucking see you again! What the fuck is wrong with you?! You're a goddamn fucking idiot sometimes! How the fuck are you in the gifted program when you're this fucking stupid?! You have no God damn fucking common sense."

When we got home, I got my ass beat.

By the time I walked through the doors of Skyview Elementary for fifth grade, I had no idea how to behave anymore.

~ 15 ~

FRANKLY, SCARLETT...

Of all things, I liked books best.
~ Nikola Tesla

As I'm sure you've gathered so far, I love to read. Fiction, biographies, autobiographies, self-help, true crime, give me all the books. I've read Gone with the Wind no less than a dozen times. I know there are people out there who detest Scarlett O'Hara for varying reasons, but I adore her for her tenacity, drive, and resilience. You don't get to know the true Scarlett until you read the sequel, Scarlett, wherein she travels to Ireland, actually gets her milky-white hands dirty, and raises her daughter on her own. For me, the apex of the story wasn't when Rhett came back for her, but rather watching her finally grow up and become her own person.

Even more than I love Scarlett, however, I've found a new character with whom I've become enamored: Elsa Dutton of *1883*, the prequel to the TV show, *Yellowstone*. Elsa is an eighteen year old woman, full of grit and substance, and a take-no-shit attitude. She is fearless, brave, and opinionated, and loves fiercely.

This is what fictional characters inspire in me. They provide me with success stories, watching people through words walk through the fire and come out better than before. It reaffirms that hard things can be done. That today, as bad as it may be, doesn't have to be the blueprint for the rest of our lives. Books (and some movies) with strong characters, characters that show who they really are, make me want to show who I really am. They inspire me to be true to myself, to embrace myself, and provide the freedom to walk my own path. I don't aspire to be the characters themselves, but to emulate their breakthroughs and triumphs through tribulations.

So often we think we have to contort ourselves into what other people want us to be so that they will be happy, proud of us, or to not hurt them. In effect, we are really only hurting ourselves by molding to their cookie cutter. We're keeping ourselves contained in boxes that we weren't meant to be in. We're clipping our own wings for the sake of another, instead of showing others how to fly (and if they don't want to fly, that's their freedom of choice, too!). It's safe in these boxes, in these churches, in these marriages, in these relationships, we think, because actually leaping out of the nest is fucking hard. Standing on the edge, knowing you could fall to your death, is terrifying.

But say you do fall to your death? Would you rather have it said about you that you took the leap of faith, or just stayed in your nest or box, never seeing if you actually could fly? Death is inevitable, and for me, I don't want to die wondering what could have been. What life could have been like if I had taken more chances on the things that intrigued me. Whose face I could have brought a smile to by giving them a sincere compliment. Who I may inspire to make a change in their own life because I did in mine. I will, forever and ever amen, always think of my children and what I model to them, and stagnation for the sake of conforming to society or tradition is not what I want to emulate.

~ 16 ~

DAILY PRAYERS | 2018

Just as ripples spread out when a single pebble is dropped into water,
the actions of individuals can have far-reaching effects.
~His Holiness, The Dalai Lama

I stare at him with one eye open. It's the eye that's closest to the pillow so he can't see me watching him play his game on his phone.

Who *is* this person? I glance across the room at our wedding picture on the dresser. The dog scratches herself and adjusts in her bed. There is stuff on every flat surface in this house. The bedroom smells like musty dogs. I have quit being controlling and doing what the experts say to encourage my husband to find his masculinity, but it's not working because he doesn't see the mess that I see. No wonder I'm always so anxious and frustrated. There is no order here.

I go back to staring at him. He's still good-looking to me, and since he started working out, his shoulders and biceps are full and strong. Physically, I would be attracted to him. But the burning in the pit of my stomach isn't desire. It's anger. And fear. And regret. And sadness. Because once again, I am not seen.

How could someone so nice-looking, with such kind eyes, be so selfish? How could I have made yet another big mistake in my life? How could someone so smart at his job be so dumb when it comes to me? Is it me? Am I the drama? Am I the problem? Maybe I'm too sensitive, too emotional. I should wall off how I feel and toughen up. Get a thicker skin. Not let things bother me so much.

And Lord knows, I've tried. I've tried to ignore things that people say and do. Let them be themselves. But when I try to do that for one set of people, because they're related to me by marriage, it bleeds into everyone else. I can't not care. The way his family treats me and talks to me not only shows me who they are, but it shows me what they think of me, and if that many people dislike me, maybe I'm unlikeable?

I continue staring. I want to reach out and touch him,but if I touch him, he'll think I want sex, and sex is the last thing I want. What I want is for him to *see* me. He doesn't have to understand me, I barely understand myself sometimes, but see me. What bothers me, what hurts me, what interests me. I want him to say, I love how much you love literally everyone. I love how you care for everyone. I love how reliable, dependable and kind you are. I love how persistent you are, and how idealistic you are. Instead, what he says is, "You spend too much time with the kids", "You spend too much time on everyone else", "You spend too much time worrying about the world's problems"...and "You're too smart for your own good".

What he doesn't understand is that everyone else **is** part of our world. How we care for others, especially our kids, bleeds into the world and creates a ripple effect. We are supposed to be the hands and feet. If we keep burying our heads in the sand, nothing changes.

I want to poke him in his eye. I want to punch him in his nose. I want to take an electric shock device and wake up the empathetic portion of his brain. We could be great together, with his brains and my ideas. Why didn't any of my good qualities rub off on him? His did on me. I became more responsible, more reliable, less flaky, less fly-off-the-handle. I stayed for 20 years instead of bolting like I usually do. But it seems nothing of me has rubbed off onto him.

I close my eyes, and say the same damn prayer I've prayed almost daily for the last 20 years.

God, please just tell me what to do.

MEDIOCRITY | 2014

Everyone, either from modesty or egotism, hides away the best and most delicate of his soul's possessions; to gain the esteem of others, we must only ever show our ugliest sides; this is how we keep ourselves on the common level.
~ Gustave Flaubert

It's easy to be mediocre. Don't shoot me, hear me out.

Striving to be the best version of yourself is hard work, and not something that many people are willing to do. It requires forethought in your actions, it requires planning, it requires dedication, and it requires working together with others. Mediocrity, on the other hand, simply requires that you be content with where you are, with no desire to change. Everyone has their own definition of mediocre and excellence. My definition of mediocrity is wasted potential, while sitting on your couch complaining that everyone else has "all the luck". Most of the time it isn't luck, it's hard work. Sure, some people may have a financial or ability advantage, but for the vast majority of Americans, there's not many reasons why we can't be and do better.

My definition of excellence is always seeking to improve your life and those around you. I know this isn't the easiest pill to swallow, but we can always do better. When we leave things up to other people, things may not always get done. If everyone had that attitude, nothing would get done, we would all be sitting around pointing fingers at each other, saying, "This is your responsibility, you can take care of this".

Worse still, are those who accept mediocrity for themselves, but armchair quarterback other's lives. Sometimes it comes from a place of wanting what's best for our children, hoping they learn from our mistakes, and do better than we did, but what we fail to remember is that children more often model what we do, not what we say. If we are not demonstrating that we are attempting to achieve the "better" that we wish for them, all we're modeling is mediocrity. "I want this for you, but I'm not willing to work for it, hope you do".

Our words and our actions need to line up in order to be good examples for children and the people around us.

When we make excuses for why we didn't do things or behave better, we're exampling that to get through life, you can coast on excuses. When we say one thing, yet do another, we're exampling that our word means nothing.

It's difficult to get up from the comfort of our "good enough". Fear of failure is a paralyzing concept. It can be devastating to try your hardest at something, sinking time and money into it, and have it not succeed. We feel like if we fail at something, we're not good enough. What's actually the truth is that you're more than good enough, you're amazing *because* you tried! If babies quit trying to walk after the first time they fell, none of us would ever be walking. Failing provides learning opportunities to discover what we like, what we're good at, how we can do better next time. Maybe we learn to delegate some things, maybe we learn that we need to be more aware, maybe we learn that through mistakes that we're actually good at something all together different.

Trying and failing can also boost your self-esteem, believe it or not. Character is built, fortitude is built, resilience is built. It gives you the opportunity to learn your own strengths and weaknesses. If you attempt something that you think you're not good at anyway, you might be surprised that you're better at it than you think. Or you learn a different way to approach it. Every time we attempt something new, we increase our chances of being better, or finding out at what we excel.

Most people opt to remain average. It's the "norm". It's easier to sit around and discuss the latest TV binge series or who said what on social media than to discuss mental health, self-growth, or entrepreneurship.

Mediocrity is also demonstrated in having too loose or blind goals. "I want to go to Fiji one day" will never happen without a solid plan. Have you researched what it would take to make that dream happen? "I would love to own my own business, but I just don't have what it takes" is a cop-out. We all know the stories of where Bezos, Jobs and Gates started off. What makes you think you can't do it, too?

More than likely it's laziness, complacency, fear, or a combination of all three. I know that sounds extremely harsh and critical, but it's the truth. Either stop making excuses, or stop judging those who are putting in the work and lamenting how bad you have it. If you're happy with where you are, your sitting back and telling everyone else how they could be doing something better does nothing. No one wants to hear the opinions of someone who hasn't even made the slightest attempt to better themselves. It's easy to tell someone they need to be on anti-depressants if they're dealing with *your* bullshit. It's easy to tell someone they need to be in therapy if you've never made any attempt to help them out or listened to their story. It's easy to judge another, because it makes you feel better about your complacency.

Hear that again. It's easy to judge another, because it makes you feel better about your complacency.

If you're doing nothing, you won't make any mistakes. You won't fail, you won't falter. So when someone else is out there doing the work, and you call them out on their mistakes, it's really you that looks like an asshole.

Let the haters fuel the fire in you to keep going.

> If everyone is pleased with what you're doing or saying, you're not saying what needs to be said.

~ 18 ~

DO AS I SAY, NOT AS I DO | 2010

I have seen parents so heap rules on their children, that it was impossible for the poor little ones to remember a tenth part of them, much less to observe them...Let therefore your rules to your son be as few as possible, and rather fewer than more seem absolutely necessary.
~John Locke

Often, parents will use some rendering of the phrase, "Do as I say, not as I do" in admonition to their children. I know I heard it growing up. On one hand, it seems to make sense: parents don't wish for their children to make the same mistakes they did, and/or parents as adults use this as an entitlement to be able to do as they please and maintain control of their children. There are definitely things adults can do that children can't, so the phrase could be used as long as it's within certain realms of context. On the other hand, if the phrase is used as a control measure, where adults feel they can arbitrarily do whatever they wish, and then off-handedly tell their children "there's nothing to see here", then it becomes hypocritical.

Children emulate their parents, and hearing "Do as I say not as I do" isn't an effective way to model how children should behave. It teaches them nothing but the ability to dismiss poor behavior.

Let's take a look from where the phrase originated, because historically, phrases have been shortened, changed and bastardized through generations that we today take almost as gospel (such as, "Blood is thicker than water").

On June 24, 1911, The Spectator gave this advice: "It has always been considered allowable to say to children, 'Do as I say, rather than as I do.'" This phrase goes back several generations before, however. In John Selden's book Table Talk (written in 1654 just before his death), he writes: ""Preachers say, "Do as I say, not as I do.'" In 1546, John Heywood wrote in "A Dialogue Containing the Number of the Effectual Proverbs in the English Tongue", "It is as folke dooe, and not as folke say." In another version of the same book, it says, "Do that he doeth not, as old men have told."

Going back even further in time, Anglo-Saxons in the 12th Century used the phrase, *"Ac theah ic wyrs do thonne ic the lære ne do thu na swa swa ic do, ac do swa ic the lære gyf ic the wel lære"* which translates into: *"Although I do worse than I teach you, do not do as I do, but do as I teach you if I teach you well."* (The Concise Oxford Dictionary of Proverbs, Oxford University Press, 2003) To me, this lends a humanistic approach: Sometimes I'm going to mess up, but if I'm teaching you well (including admitting when we make mistakes, apologizing when we are wrong, and telling of lessons we've learned through life via our mistakes), hopefully, the next generations will do better.

Essentially, this phrase can be traced back to Jesus in Matthew 23:1-4, where he says, "The teachers of the law and the Pharisees sit in Moses' seat. So you must be careful to do everything they tell you. But do not do what they do, for they do not practice what they preach. They tie up heavy, cumbersome loads and put them on other people's shoulders, but they themselves are not willing to lift a finger to move them..."

See how over time the original phrase gets turned backwards, and out of context? Jesus, purportedly the originator of this proverb, was telling the people that the Pharisees, who were well-known to be pompous show-boaters, chose to just preach what should be done but didn't put it to practice.

Ultimately, this phrase is simply telling children (or others) follow my instructions and ignore the example I am setting.

Control.

Patriarchy.

Protecting men.

Protecting the white.

Far too often, parents expect their children to provide a better example to the world than themselves. And don't get me started on parents living vicariously through their children. We discipline children backwards: chastising them in public, and praising them (if we even do) in private. Children are not just short adults, but they are also, at times, much wiser than adults because of their innocence. They don't yet know the rules the establishment has placed on society, and question why things are the way they are. Instead of reflecting on the candid lucidity of their questions, we simply tell them to go along with what we say, "because I said so".

~ 19 ~

1986

Death, they say, acquits us of all obligations.
~Michel Eyquem de Montaigne

I was so glad to have a day off from school. Even better, I was going to a friend's house, so I wouldn't have to spend the day off with my father. I was awake, getting ready, my mother was getting ready for work, when there was a knock at our front door. No one ever came to our front door, so this had to be a salesperson, or a Jehovah's Witness who didn't know we were, also. My mom answered the door, and I heard her speaking quietly to the person, then she called me to the living room.

It was a woman, dressed in business attire. She asked if I knew why she was there. Nope. She said they had received a concerning call about an incident. I was clueless. I ran through my brain, trying to recall if I had done something stupid at school, and nothing came up. She rephrased. An incident with my father. My mom looked at me, and I panicked.

My father walked through the back door.

The woman asked him if he knew about an incident that had occurred between he and I, and he denied it. She then asked my mom what our plans were for the day, and my mom replied that she was going to work, and I was going to a friend's. The woman left. My mom left for work.

My father didn't speak a word to me. I went back into my room, awaiting what was coming, but it never came. My friend and her mom came to pick me up, and we went to their house. I was there less than two hours when another woman came to their door. She said she needed to pick me up and take me to my grandmother's. Sister Baker came in and told me my mom knew I was supposed to go with this woman, so I did. But we didn't go to my grandmother's. We went to an office, where they asked me again if I remembered an incident with my father. I said no. They said they had gotten a call from a woman named Gail, did I know her? Yes, she's my great aunt. Did I remember telling her anything?

I loved Auntie Gail more than any other family member. She had moved to Florida from Boston, and I was thrilled to have her nearby. We would make candles, and bake, watch Andre Agassi play tennis and gawk at how cute he was. Her apartment was filled with plants, and she always smelled like sweat and Downy. She made the best sun tea, using Constant Comment and orange juice; and her homemade pizza was to die for.

We'd had a sleepover, as we often did, and this night in particular I was upset with my father. Our house was being tented for termites, and my Gramma lent us her pop-up trailer to put in our front yard, so we would have a place to sleep. I was helping my father set up the trailer before my mom came home from work. My brother and his friends were running in and out as little boys are wont to do, acting rambunctious. It was going to be a crowded weekend. I told my father, "Why don't I just stay at Gramma's or Auntie Gail's so I'm not in the way, and there's less people underfoot?" He told me to get the fuck out. I was a princess, and was too good to stay in a trailer, so I might as well just move out. He threw my clothes out the door of the trailer and told me not to come back. This wasn't the first time he had thrown my clothes out and told me to leave, so I shrugged my shoulders, went in the house, and called my Gramma to take me to Auntie Gail's. When I hung up, he slapped me for shrugging my shoulders. His outbursts were less frequent than before, but I was sick of it. Later that evening, as I lay on the couch getting ready to go to sleep at Auntie Gail's, I asked her, "Is it okay if your father touches you? Is that rape?"

She had promised not to tell anyone, because as far as I could remember, it had only happened that summer. He wasn't drinking as much anymore, and he had a job. He wasn't running with the Indians as much after he almost burned the house down, so things were semi-calm.

She turned my whole world upside down.

I was asked to tell the story three times that day, to three different people. They told me I couldn't go home. I didn't want to go back to Auntie Gail's ever again, she had betrayed me and not even given me a heads-up. My grandmother was at work, so I went to Gail's daughter's house. I didn't like Cheryl. She was mean to Gail and my grandmother, and she was bossy. But there was no where else for me to go. They must have told her what was going on, because she was the nicest to me she's ever been that afternoon.

My grandmother came to get me that evening, bringing me some clothes from the house, but nothing that I wanted. I didn't have much to choose from to begin with. When we got to her house, she was all over me, hugging me, pulling me close, crying. "I wish Grampa was here. I can't believe his little girl has to go through this!" I had to console her, and tell her everything was fine, I was fine, it was going to be fine.

She drove me to my bus stop that next morning for school, and I was never in my life so happy to see my bus friend Eve.

My mom, grandmother, and Auntie Gail decided that I would stay with my grandmother during the week, and with Auntie Gail on the weekends. That was fine by me, because my grandmother was very strict, and frugal. She would get upset with me for my appetite, frustrated when on Fridays, we would stop at Subway, I wanted a footlong instead of a six-inch sub. Auntie Gail had no problems with feeding me, and I could eat as much as I wanted. She also had better food, and was a much better cook. The first Friday I arrived at Auntie Gail's, I was furious with her for betraying my trust. She told me she had a moral obligation to do so, and while I was angry, I understood.

Later, I would learn that a rift formed between Gramma and Auntie Gail, because they both wanted me to live with them full-time. They both believed they were the best choice for me during this time. I loved my Gramma dearly, but living with her was difficult for a 14-year-old. She woke me up in the mornings, flipping on the bright overhead light, clapping her hands, and yanking the covers off me. Auntie Gail was a night owl like me, so we stayed up watching TV, talking, or playing games. Ultimately, it ended up being the best of both worlds, they were happy to have time with me, and I got the discipline and structure I'm sure I needed. However, it became a chore having to console my grandmother when it was my time of need.

I was assigned a Guardian Ad Litem, Barbara, and I adored her. She had this awesome blue convertible, and she would pick me up, and take me to counseling appointments, or we would just drive around and talk. She had cropped red hair, and an overbite that I was fascinated by. She was my mom's age, but seemed so much cooler. I don't know if she knows how much she meant to me, or how much I needed someone like her, but she really made an impact on me.

One evening after the meeting, I insisted that my Gramma drive me to my mom's house. I didn't get to see her much, except at the meetings, and I wanted more of my clothes, and things from my room. It had been about two weeks, and it didn't look like I was going home anytime soon. Barbara had told me that I couldn't go home until my father had moved out. My mom told me that he had moved out, so I was confused as to why I wasn't able to go home. We pulled up to the house, and my Gramma told me I couldn't go to the door, she would have to go. Furious, I jumped out of the car before she could, and banged on the back door. My mom answered, and I tried to shove my way in, but she blocked me. "Why can't I go in my own house?!" I yelled. "Is he here?" She said no, so I tried to shove again. My little brother peeked his head around the doorway, and I asked him, "Is he here?!" He went to his room. "If he's not here, I can come inside. They told me I could come home if you make him leave! Why haven't you made him leave?!" My mom quietly asked me what I needed, and she would get it for me. "I HATE YOU!" I yelled, and went back to the car.

When I saw Barbara a couple days later, I asked her if she knew whether my father was still living at home. She said yes. My mother was a liar. I called her and asked her why she had lied to me, and why was he still living there? Why didn't she want her daughter home? Why was she choosing him over me? Did she not believe me? "Its complicated", she said. "Complicated, my ass! You're choosing him over me. Why don't you believe me?" She told me there was a lot I didn't understand, and that was the end of the discussion. I hated my mother for years after that, so Barbara and Auntie Gail became my stand-in mothers.

Counseling was a joke, to say the least. We had group therapy sessions, during which time we used to bitch about everything and nothing. We rarely talked about the issues for why we were there. It was state-mandated, though, and the sessions were all over the county. I felt like I was constantly in the car. Individual sessions were a little better, although I was already sick of talking about what had happened. I had to repeat the story over and over so the counselors and attorneys could verify I was telling the truth. Was it Wesson or Mazola oil? What color was the nightgown? Where was your brother? Why didn't you say anything sooner? Are you angry with your father, and trying to get revenge? Was he drunk? Do you know if he was using drugs? Why do you think he didn't have actual sex with you? One afternoon, I heard my name called over the school loudspeakers to come to the office. There waiting was a woman from the state, to take me to my very first gynecology appointment. My virginity was being questioned. Fortunately, I was rendered intact, and still very much a virgin, so at least I had that going for me.

It was August before I was able to return home. I don't know when my father had finally left the house, but while I was gone, my mom had adopted a dog, and I could tell my father had been sleeping in my bed. It didn't even feel like home anymore. My brother and I picked up where we had left off, him being annoying and ten, and me being bossy and fourteen. He had some new friends, and I taught them how to pick the padlock on the back of the cable box so they could watch HBO after 9 pm. At least I was still the big sister.

My mom and I fought often. I was resentful. I could have been home long before, but she chose that asshole over her own kid. The man who had hit her, cheated on her, was a drunk, in and out of rehab, cussed at her and her kids, almost burned her house down, couldn't keep a job. That's who she chose. She repulsed me. I vowed never to be anything like her, I would always choose my children over any man.

One day, a letter addressed to me came in the mail. I didn't recognize the writing, but opened it anyway. Inside was a letter from someone named Jim, telling me that my father missed me, and if I wanted to write to him, I could, at the given address. Wanting answers from someone, and curious to see what he had to say, I wrote to him. I told him about my first boyfriend, John, and that I wasn't looking forward to high school because I wasn't going where my friends were going. I was still in the gifted program, by the skin of my teeth at this point, and it was only offered at one school in our district. He wrote back almost immediately. In the letter, he half admitted to what he had done, saying it was for "educational purposes". He was trying to teach me how a man should treat me, how I should enjoy myself, and educate myself to protect my body.

I was pissed. I turned the letter over to Barbara, who turned it over to the state. There was the proof, in his own handwriting. He was put in jail.

My mom was upset that I had turned the letter over without telling her. Because he was in jail, he was now unemployed, and couldn't send money to us. She said that was why she hadn't made him leave the house, he had told her he wouldn't give her money if she threw him out. I didn't care. It was the principle.

He wrote me again from jail, pleading for me to tell the state I had lied. He said I had all the power, and I could bring the family back together. He said it was all a misunderstanding, and didn't I want to be in control? If I told them I had lied, he would be indebted to me, and I could have anything I wanted, I could be the boss of the house if I wanted. He told me how smart I was, and that he would entrust me with running the finances, the chores, everything. The family would be at my behest. He went on to say that I would regret starving my mom and little brother, because now he couldn't provide for us. We would lose the house, and our car. Did I want to be responsible for that?

I turned that letter in as well.

Right before school started, I was home alone, reading. Someone rattled the handle on the back door. Surprisingly, it was locked. Then there was a knock at the front door. Our doors were frosted jalousie, so there was no way to see who was outside. I opened the door a crack, and there was my father. He asked to be let in, and I said no. As I was closing the door, he pushed against it, but I pushed harder, and locked it. I was trapped. My mom had grounded me, and had taken the phone with her. I couldn't call the police. He stood outside the door, telling me how sorry he was, how much he loved me. He told me he was sober now. He wanted our family back together. Didn't I miss our family? Tears streamed down my face. For a brief moment, I considered opening the door. I would tell the state I had lied. We could try being a family again. He then said I was killing him, his only daughter had ripped his heart out, and shredded it. "His only daughter". That dried up the tears. He had a daughter from a previous marriage, Michelle. I wasn't his only daughter. I didn't know the word for it then, but he was manipulating me. I told him to go away before I called the police, that I didn't want to see him. I told him I loved him, but he needed help, and our family was horrible because he was a drunk. "Go to jail, serve your time, get sobered up, and then maybe we can talk," I told him. He walked away, got into a car, and drove off. As he was driving away, my brother was coming home. He called out for my father, but he didn't hear him. My brother came inside, and asked why I hadn't let him in. I told him that he wasn't allowed to be here. He went outside, slamming the door behind him, yelling "You ruined our family!"

When my mom came home with the phone, I called Barbara and told her what had transpired. She said she would let the authorities know. My father went back to jail. Now we were really hurting financially, and I felt like everyone hated me. Group sessions were still ridiculously a waste of time, I didn't like my individual counselor, and I didn't want to confide what was going on with my boyfriend. I felt like I was walking on landmines, and Barbara was the only one I could trust.

Grocery shopping day was like Christmas to me. We suddenly went from empty cabinets to what seemed like a full-on buffet. Having a full refrigerator was extremely satisfying to look at, but by mid-week, it was bare again. My mom would make back-handed comments about how much we ate, but we weren't wasteful eaters. We ate what we served ourselves. I knew a lot of people who would throw away the heels of a loaf of bread or pizza crusts, but I always made sure to eat everything. When it was time to go back to school, my mom was very specific about what we could buy. One coat for winter, one pair of shoes, three shirts, and one pair of jeans. I picked out a pale yellow, thick coat with a knit collar, and made sure to wear it all through high school.

I started ninth grade at Northeast High. The kids in my neighborhood were all bussed across town to Gibbs, so I walked if the weather was good, or my mom drove me if it was raining. We started to get along a little better and weren't fighting as much. I would wake up at 6 am, do a workout with Denise Austin, and go to school. I knew no one, and didn't make any attempts to make friends. My middle school bus friend, Eve, was at Gibbs, so I just stayed to myself. At lunch, I would sit in the library and read. At home, I would stay on the phone for hours with John. My grades plummeted. By the end of the first semester, I had failed almost every single class, was expelled from the gifted program, and was sent to Gibbs.

Because I was wasting so much time on the phone, and my mom was having a hard time keeping us fed, she helped me get a job in the mall at an ice cream shop. I loved my job. I thought I was big time, getting paid $3.35 an hour. I could actually buy my own food, or clothes that I wanted.

One Sunday, after the meeting, my mom dropped me off at work. She picked me up after my shift, and we drove home in silence. I could tell something was wrong, and I assumed I was in trouble. Shortly after we got home, one of the brothers from our congregation, Brother Larry, came over. We had known him since I was little, I loved his wife, and had a huge crush on his oldest son, Carey, for years. Sometimes the brothers would make visits to families to check in on them, so I didn't think anything of it, until he had my brother and I sit at the kitchen table with him and my mom. I chose instead to sit on the yellow stool at the counter. Something in the house smelled funny, sour almost. Rancid.

Brother Larry was one of the kindest men I knew. He was soft spoken, and had a pleasant face. He was always one of my favorite brothers at the congregation, next to Brother Theodore, who was funny, boisterous, and teasing. I could tell Brother Larry had something important to tell us from the way he was talking to my brother and me. He was treating us with kid gloves.

My mom and brother had come home after dropping me off at the mall for work. My brother's friend, Joey, was standing in the driveway, waiting for them. He told my mom, "Something happened to your husband." He and my brother then ran off to play down the street. My mom called Joey's mom, and she told her that my father had collapsed on the street and the ambulance had taken him to the hospital, but she didn't know which one. My mom then called the local hospitals and found him. They told her to come in. She went in, and the curtain was partially open. She saw my father's hand, with the shield tattoo on the back. "It's him," she told them, and left.

My father was dead.

~ 20 ~

MYRTLE NECK, PART TWO | 1980

The Primordial Power is ever at play. She is creating, and destroying in play, as it were. This power is called Kali.
~Ramakrishna

In our new rental house, I am so excited for the cherry turnovers my mom has bought for our first morning's breakfast. I love new adventures of any kind. My brother and I each have our own rooms for the first time. We've lived in my grandparent's house for well over 6 months, and now that my Grampa has passed away, I feel we've overstayed our welcome, especially since I blame myself for his death.

My brother and I had been our usual annoying selves, me ever the instigator. My Gramma is in the kitchen, cleaning, of course. I was sitting on my Grampa's lap, my brother on the floor, when I look up at him and see his eyes closed. "Wake up, Grampa", I say. It's too early for bed. "Gramma!! Grampa is playing asleep and won't wake up! Tell him to wake up!" I'm not concerned at all, I just think he's playing a game to get us to be quiet. My Gramma comes running into the living room, and we are immediately sent to our

69

room. My brother and I look at each other, completely confused, but we know that tone, and when it's time to obey. There is a rush of energy that comes from the living room, and suddenly we hear sirens in the distance. Everything becomes a blur from that moment, but we remain hiding in our shared room. The paramedics come in and there is a lot of talking, but we can't hear what's going on. Grampa is taken to the hospital, a place that so far in my almost nine years, everyone returns from, so I'm not concerned.

But he never comes home.

Sitting in the kingdom hall at his service, I'm in the middle section, someplace I don't usually sit. I tell myself that I'm supposed to be brave, and not cry. I'm supposed to be stoic and strong. My best friend, Sheila, sits next to me. Her eyes are filled with tears, and she holds my hand. I comfort her, still not completely grasping what all this means, how I'm supposed to act, and if anyone knows I killed my grandfather. If I hadn't been so damn loud, if I didn't talk so much, if I didn't egg my brother on, he would still be here. I'm sure my grandmother has told everyone that if it weren't for me, he would still be here. I decide then and there to just keep my big mouth shut.

My brother quickly makes friends in our new neighborhood, and I befriend our next door neighbor, Jolene. She's younger than me, but she's really the only girl to play with. We get along for the most part, but she's such a girl, whiny and dramatic, and a big crybaby. I would much rather play with my brother and his friends, building tree forts and riding bikes, throwing rocks and sticks, and playing in the ditch. I watch them climb the roofs of the houses and jump off. They build fires and catch lizards. My brother is less interested in me now that he has friends, so I sit in the tree fort we built together and read books about girls who have great adventures like Trixie Belden, and girls who don't quite fit in, like most of the girls in Judy Blume's books.

At school, I want to play kickball and football with the boys, but by fourth grade, they just want to be my boyfriend. I agree to be Fat

Boy's girlfriend, just so I can run around with the boys, and then he tries to kiss me. I break up with him, and he is furious. He backs me up against a wall of one of the houses and yells at me. I strangely feel exhilarated. I shove him away from me, kicking him in the shin. We don't speak again until he moves away and apologizes.

In fifth grade, Jacob Loomy passes me notes in class. He wants to be my boyfriend, too. I tell him I'll be his girlfriend if he lets me play kickball with them at recess. I had been shunned from playing with them before this, so when he agrees, I'm ecstatic. Finally. I can play outside and not sit against the wall or pick flowers with the girls. When it's recess, I try not to show my excitement, and walk over to the kickball field. We start to play a game, and then the boys decide they want to play football instead. Since I'm now Jacob's girlfriend, I assume I can play football with the boys. I catch the ball, and Jacob runs beside me, snatching the ball from my arms. He's not supposed to do this because we are on the same team, and I was going to make the touchdown. I run after him, tackle him to the ground, and punch him in his face.

Jacob and I spend the rest of the school year breaking up when he won't let me play with the boys, and getting back together when he promises to let me join. I'm already sick of the cat and mouse game that seems to be required of tomboys like me, and I'm sick of the women at the kingdom hall who are already expecting me to be ladylike and stop wanting to play. I get chastised weekly by one particular sister who has two perfect daughters. I get their hand me down clothes and toys, dolls and ruffles, and she tries to bribe me with a manicure set if I stop picking my nails. I can't stop. I'm a nervous wreck now that my father has moved from Connecticut to be with us.

After the incident with my father, I decide that apparently all boys want is one thing. It's ridiculous, and I'm both heartbroken and angry. All I want to do is play and have fun. Why, at age ten, am I already expected to be a lady? And who decided that being a lady entails dresses, ruffles, lipstick and nail polish? I start reading my mother's Women's Day magazines, to figure out how I'm supposed to be a girl. One of them has a test you can take to determine what kind of woman you are. Unquestionably, my results come back as "guy's girl".

~ 21 ~

BIRACIAL | 2019

*If you are neutral in situations of injustice, you have chosen the side of
the oppressor.*
~Desmond Tutu

*To be African American is to be African without any memory, and
American without any privilege.*
~James Baldwin

I am probably the whitest biracial person you will ever meet. I rarely use the term biracial, because I never wanted to seem as if I was taking anything away from the experience that black people have had to endure. Because I'm so light skinned, it seemed unfair to claim any blackness because I experienced white privilege all my life. It felt like I was trying to show a sort of golden ticket to force my way into a club or an allyship with my black friends to say "Oh yeah I'm black too". I didn't feel I deserved to make that announcement early on because I didn't have to experience racism of any sort. My blood may be black, my soul may have black in it, but my experiences don't align with either fact.

73

When I was in 7th grade, I made fun of a boy on the bus along with other kids. His older sister was rightly pissed off, and threatened to beat my ass. I went home that day, scared to death, and my father asked me what was wrong. I told him. He beat my ass for making fun of the kid. But the next morning, he walked me to the bus stop and got on the bus and handed the older sister a letter. He said, before you fight my daughter, read this.

She never told me what the letter said, and neither would my father, but she did say that she was sorry for me too because I was part black. This was the first time I had ever heard my father acknowledge his true heritage. My father's skin color got me out of getting my ass deservedly beaten a second time.

I never wanted that to give me a pass again. It didn't seem fair.

Growing up, my father convinced us that he was American Indian. As I got older, I suspected this was a lie because I knew he had been married before, and my half brothers and sister were black. His birth certificate listed his race as "Colored", as did his Army enlistment papers. His discharge papers list him as American Indian, and it's still a mystery to me how he was able to change his ethnicity on those records. I later learned he claimed to be American Indian because he kept getting denied disability from the VA, and he thought that being American Indian would get him more voice than being black. While I understand his need to be heard and receive disability benefits, I never liked that he denied his heritage and used another one to get ahead. I tried to avoid this behavior in myself.

When I was seventeen, I overheard on the news about a black toddler getting shot in a drive-by while he was sleeping in his bed. The bullet went through the wall of his apartment and killed him. I wanted to throw up. While I had grown up poor, and we lived in government housing, and had WIC, I don't think my parents ever had to worry about my safety in drive-by shootings.

Years later, I started getting jobs. There was, on more than one occasion, that I later learned I got the job because I was pretty. I confronted one of my employers about it, and of course, he denied it, but I knew the truth. I wondered if I would have gotten the job if I was overweight....or black.

When Hurricane Katrina hit in 2005, I remember hearing on the news about how people were being packed into the Superdome and some were being raped. Houses were destroyed. Businesses and communities were lost forever, and families had to completely relocate. I was devastated for them. I knew that white people experienced this, too, but I also knew that white people probably carried more insurance to cover their needs, and were less likely to be taken advantage of and overlooked in these situations. I sat in my daughter's closet, crying, when seeing news report after news report aired about the horrendous tragedy. How is this fair? Why is there such disparity?

When I finally met my half-sister in August 2018, we each talked about how our experiences were so different, despite having the same father. The father she had was proud of his black heritage and musical talent. The father I had was in denial of his heritage and was a heroin and alcohol addict.

I find myself avoiding conversations with her regarding race because even though we have the common bond of our father, I feel shame that we didn't have even remotely the same experiences. I know what it's like to be an outcast for sure, because I never quite knew who I was or where I fit in, but being so light skinned opened doors for me that even the most confident black person would probably not have access to. She and I are able to have brief conversations about the injustices when George Floyd and Ahmaud Arbery are blatantly murdered, and even though I am incensed, it still doesn't feel that she believes I'm on her side. Rightly so. White people have been historically known for using black people to give substance to their platforms, and then quickly disappear when they get what they want (Susan B. Anthony, anyone?). I futilely argue with others on social media about the unfairness of how persons of color are treated. It's so easy for certain people to dismiss the in-our-face facts, even when I've implored them to watch shows such as *13th*, or read books from authors such as Audre Lorde or Ijeoma Oluo. They argue back that they weren't the ones who brought slaves over, or "What about Affirmative Action?", but they fail to recognize that these comments are still coming from a place of high privilege. They refuse to educate themselves or look in a mirror...because they fear they might lose something that was stolen from the start. Even as recent as a few days ago, on the anniversary of #metoo, pretty while girl Alyssa Milano has been given false credit for the movement. Why is it that when Tarana Burke started the movement, it took five years and a white woman to make it mean something?

The comedian Paul Mooney once said that white people have the complexion for the (privilege of) the protection. So why aren't we using our platform of privilege to create protection, and amplify their voices? Why are their words, stories, and work being appropriated? And at the very least, we should be creating protection by shutting down racism in our homes. "But I like black people!", "I'm not racist!" you cry. Are you giving ole Poppy Bill a pass for using racist terminology because "he's old and doesn't know better"? We need to stop putting old white men in these exclusive positions of power and respect when they aren't earning it.

Again, I ask, *how is this fair? Why is there such disparity?*

~ 22 ~

MYRTLE NECK, PART THREE | 2020

When I look at my brother, I no longer see my past. I see strength and endurance. I see someone who shares my blood. When I look at him, I fill with pride, because in seeing him, I see myself. We made it.
~s. kilata

My mom is now working full time, at Florida Federal Bank. My brother and I are shuffled around from babysitter to babysitter, not because we misbehave, but because my mom has to ask favors from people to watch us so she doesn't have to pay for someone full time. One afternoon, we're at the Larry's house, and I have had a crush on their son, Carey, since I laid eyes on him when I was six. He's outside playing baseball, and I ask if I can play, too. He says yes, he needs someone to pitch to him because it's hard to pitch to yourself. I throw to him a few times, and he is impressed. I'm not only happy because I like him, but because he sees me as an equal, and not some dumb girl. He tells me to throw another pitch, and the bat meets the ball perfectly, the crack is satisfyingly loud, and he hits a perfect line drive, to my stomach.

The wind is knocked right out of me, and I double over, still standing. Carey runs over to me, in a panic. "Are you okay??? Are you okay?? Don't cry, oh my gosh, I am so sorry!!" I stand straight, not a tear in my eyes. He looks at me quizzically. I take a deep breath in, exhale, and say, "That was a great hit!" Carey stares at me, dumbfounded. When he is finally able to speak, he says, "You are the only girl I know who wouldn't be crying her eyes out after that hit. Dang, I don't even know many guys who could take that!" He is visibly in awe. My work here is done. I am a guy's girl.

The next years with my brother are a blur. He is still the light of my life, but I realize my place is not his place. I desperately want to be with him and his friends, but I stay back. When he has friends over to the house, I listen from my room as they play video games or crack jokes. I envy their ability to just be free and wild. When he is outside playing, I watch from my window or my tree fort. On occasion, I am able to entice him to hang out with me when I start throwing grapefruits at cars that pass by my tree fort. But mostly, we just dance outside each other's perimeters. One day, he and a friend are across the street playing on a massive pile of dirt and rocks. They climb up and slide down. I want to do it, too, but I know I'm not welcome. I have to be a girl. I stand in the driveway, watching, when out of the blue, his friend throws a baseball sized rock at me. It hits me square in the head, and I crumple, sitting on the ground. My brother runs over to check on me, and I say I'm ok. He spins around to his friend, and yells, "That's my SISTER!", and punches him. From that moment on, I knew that even though we couldn't run in the same circles, my brother loved me and had my back.

Today, at age forty-nine and change, I still know my brother has my back. He doesn't seem to need me to have his, but he knows I do. For the longest time, I felt like he viewed me as gullible, naïve, and incapable. I am all those things at times, but it surprises me when he takes my daughter aside one day and tells her what I've felt my whole life: that I've had to play into a role that was forced on me from a very young age. He knows that I would have much rather been setting things on fire with him than playing with dolls and chasing boys. He tells her that I've had to behave as if the only way to play their game, was to be gullible, naive and incapable. Maybe he does recognize that under the facade of this inept sister he took the task of taking care of, is someone as equally as fierce as he.

But what he doesn't know is that I adore the hell out of him, admire him, am proud of him, and still want him as my best friend. As much as I've wanted my mom's approval, his has been the one I've most chased after.

~ 23 ~

HE SPOKE IT UNTIL IT BECAME TRUTH | 2019

And those who were seen dancing were thought to be insane by those
who could not hear the music.
~Friedrich Nietzsche

I'm pretty confident in my abilities when I set out to do something, despite myself, despite the weird looks and comments about the ideas I come up with. The problem is that I shut down most of the ideas I have, because of myself, because of the weird looks and comments I get about them. Not all the things I set out to do are successful, but at least I can say I tried. Isn't that what life is about? Trying, failing, seeing what works and what doesn't? Isn't that how we have progressed as a society, as humankind?

I don't tell all my ideas to everyone most of the time. I just do them, see what sticks, and move on.

In my idea of marriage, however, you're supposed to be able to share all your hair-brained ideas with your partner. And in my idea of marriage, your partner is supposed to encourage you to try it; and if it works, they praise you, and if it fails, they support you.

When my oldest was a baby, I stayed glued to the BabyCenter message boards. It's where I met my good friend, Amanda, whose daughter was born two weeks before my son. It was on the message boards that I learned about attachment parenting and cloth diapers. I researched all about both, and decided that they were things I wanted to have in my parenting toolbox.

I was already an advocate of cloth menstrual pads, so it would make sense that cloth diapers were a much better alternative to disposable, both for the environment and the health of my baby. Being that I was a stay at home mom, and we were pretty broke, I decided that I would sew my own cloth diapers. My mom had taught me to sew at an early age, and I sewed a lot of my clothes during middle and high school (I wish I had a picture of the peppermint pink striped jumpsuit I made in 8th grade...fashion tragedy!), so I knew I could do it.

This was met with what was now becoming the usual weird look, and comments that eluded to the fact that I didn't know what I was talking about. No one else he knew used cloth diapers except maybe our grandparents. Why was I always trying to reinvent the wheel and be different?

So I sewed diapers. And wipes. And made my own diaper wipe solution. And started selling them on the internet. I didn't sell many, because they were expensive to make, but I was proud of myself.

When my daughter was born, huge bows, the size of a baby's head, were all the rage. Gymboree was popular, and having intricate, matching bows for their outfits, as well as boutique-styled outfits, was plastered all over the message boards. I learned how to make bows, starting with my daughter and niece, and added them to a new online store I created.

Again, the weird looks, this time less than with the diapers, but still...

The bows were a lot more successful than the diapers, and again, I was proud of myself for proving him wrong.

But the initial comments were still pricking at my soul. Was there anything he was going to encourage? Was there any idea I was going to have that would make him proud of me and believe in me?

It seemed that everything I thought good of myself was questioned or the wind knocked out of my sails. I was supposed to let the babies cry it out. I held them too much. I read to them too much. I danced too close to people. I was too loud. Too outspoken. Too bossy. A know it all. I used big words. I was nitpicked incessantly, a death of a thousand cuts.

I hadn't watched the news since I was in high school when a report aired about a little boy in Tampa who had been shot by a stray bullet, killing him. The news always had a way of both informing me, and frightening me to the point of being almost depressingly distraught. When the Gulf War began, I worried incessantly about my high school friends and boyfriends being drafted, nauseous at the idea of them leaving and never coming home. I was obsessed with true crime, following all the details of Lacy Peterson's disappearance, and the missing Caley Anthony, until they were eventually found, and then spent days crying about them. In August of 2005, Hurricane Katrina devastated New Orleans. The news coverage told stories of people crammed like sardines in the Dome. I sat in my daughter's closet, holding her tightly, tears streaming down my face, thinking of the children who had lost their homes and families.

I looked down at my daughter, and imagined not being able to find her. I was gripped with fear and anxiety. I sent $10, all I had access to at the time, to a fundraiser for the victims of Katrina. I packed water bottles and diaper wipes, and mailed them to another place collecting items. My husband couldn't grasp my need to help, especially when we were "broke" ourselves. But I'm a firm believer in karma, and of giving what you can when you can. Maybe it'll come back to you, maybe it won't; but knowing you could do something and didn't, was something I couldn't bear to live with.

In December of 2011, when a little girl in my local area was brutally murdered by the groundskeeper at her apartment complex, I was overcome with grief. She reminded me so much of my own daughter, carefree, brown-eyed, and innocent. One morning I woke up with the idea that I needed to create a fundraiser in her memory. I wasn't quite sure what to do with the funds, but I felt I needed to do something other than cry about her every day. My husband thought I was crazy to start a fundraiser for someone I didn't even know. "Why isn't anyone making a fundraiser for us?" he quipped. Normally, I would shove the idea into the drawer where I kept all my other shot-down proposals, but I was determined to follow through with my gut. I had to.

I contacted the organization our PTO used for a 5k. He agreed to do it, and I said, "Just bring your race equipment, give me the contact for your t-shirts, and I'll do the rest". I spent hours on the phone asking for donations from small businesses, restaurants, and local residents. I created a Facebook page, and contacted the family of the little girl, getting their permission to put on the 5k. I reached out to a foundling organization, to see if they would be interested in teaching self-defense classes to children in the local area to help prevent this type of tragedy again.

"Why would anyone come to this?" my husband asked. "No one knows you or this little girl. You're wasting your time".

For four months, I worked non-stop on this project. There was drama surrounding where the funds were actually going. There was a competing organization that created legal issues I had to figure out. At one point, I was threatened with a lawsuit. If there's one thing I am, it's tenacious.

On April 12, 2012, the sky was grey and drizzling. The planned balloon release fizzled out, the balloons unable to float into the sky. Even still, over 100 people showed up at the start line, ready to run and walk in this little girl's memory. A local radio station showed up. The newspaper did a small article on it. There was a quick video on the local TV news. And the children's self-defense organization received over $1500 as a grant to use to teach elementary-aged children how to protect themselves against predators. After the race was over, and everyone had packed up to leave, I was high. I had set out to do something, and had completed it, start to finish.

My husband never said he was proud of me, he just simply said. "I didn't think anyone would show up".

~ 24 ~

TRUST AND BELIEVE | 2021

The soul that sees beauty may sometimes walk alone.
~Johann Wolfgang von Goethe

It was hard for me to admit that what my father did impacted me more than I wanted to acknowledge. From that day forward, I lost trust in myself. I lost trust in my father, the one person I thought I was able to approach and talk to without judgement. After it all came out, I lost the rest of the trust I had in my mother.

After my father died, my mom and I continued fighting all the time. I started being even more sneaky. I skipped classes by hiding in the library, then I began skipping entire days of school. My grades plummeted. I was kicked out of the gifted program and sent to the school in which I was districted. I faltered there, too, knowing only a few people. The campus was enormous to me, and I cried in the bathroom for the first two weeks of school every morning. I tried to do better in my classes, but just wasn't making it work. My only positives were my best friend, Shelley, and my boyfriend, John.

Everyone loved Shelley, and I wanted so much to be like her. She and her mom were close, and I wanted that with my mom, too.

85

Thinking back, she and I were only five pounds different in weight, but I felt like it was a million. I stopped eating regular food, and survived on Diet Coke and apples, or tangerines from the trees in our backyard. I worked out every morning, and started running. I had control over absolutely nothing in my life, except reading.

Reading was the one place I could escape and submerge myself into stories of others. I admired the tenacity in characters, or the plots in Stephen King's novels. One day, I told myself, I will be the author of my own life, and I can be like the characters who overcame their obstacles. I started writing my own story, dreaming of the day that I would pull up to John's house (he had since broken up with me), and showing him how successful I was, and what he had missed out on.

"The book", as it became known across my high school campus, was an exaggerated version of my real life. In it, my father was my best friend, still alive, and my mom was dead. I was popular, and pretty, two things I absolutely was not in real life. People would come up to me between classes and ask me if I had written any more in "the book", and if so, could they borrow it to read. I finally felt like I had a place in the world, and excitedly kept writing. People would ask me if they could be in my book, and I would find a place for them in my story.

One day, after a big fight with my new boyfriend, Sean, who I treated like complete shit, he took my book, written on notebook paper by hand, and flung it into the air. It was windy that day, and the pages went fluttering across the quad. I scurried after them, trying to gather them up before I was late to my next class. I kept it in a binder after that, so the pages would not be so easily lost.

"The Book" was the only thing keeping me interested in school. Page after page I wrote, almost daily, attempting to rewrite my real life. I showed it to my Creative Writing teacher, and she encouraged me to apply for a summer scholarship at the Poynter Institute. I did, greedily, submitting what I thought was my best work, knowing in my soul that I would be accepted. For most of my school years, I had been praised about my writing, and this would be no different.

Finally, the letter came in the mail. I hadn't been accepted. They thanked me for applying, and better luck next time. I was disappointed, but not yet crushed. I still have the letter to this day, because upon receiving it, I meant to keep it as a dare. "You can't tell me I'm not good at writing. I'll prove to you otherwise". But I never did. Instead, I immersed myself in boys, ultimately trying to find someone else other than myself to save me. I was became focused on marriage, because once I was married, then I could settle in and live my life away from my mother and grandmother always telling me what to do, or sighing when I messed up. There was no chance for me at college, I hated school, and besides, church said that a woman's place was in the home.

If you can just find a husband, then no one will be disappointed in you anymore. Everything you've done so far, you've proven you're unreliable, untrustworthy, and not good at anything. Even your mom is ready for you to get out of her hair.

I was so desperate to be a mom so that I could do everything completely opposite of her, that I had very low standards for who I would marry. Everyone I encountered that was good looking, was my potential husband. Eventually, I met a man 15 years my senior. I was so doubtful of my own abilities, and so afraid of the power I knew I had inside myself, that I ignored all judgement, even on the day he asked me to marry him. We had gone out to dinner with another couple at a swanky restaurant. I got up to use the restroom, and when I came back, everyone made a big deal about putting their napkins in their laps. Subconsciously, I knew what was under my napkin. I didn't want it. I felt trapped. Finally, I picked up the napkin, and there was a little box. "Fuck," I thought to myself. "I can't say no and embarrass him in front of our friends". He proposed, I said yes, and immediately began thinking of ways I could sabotage the engagement, so he would break up with me. Unfortunately, according to the religion to which we then belonged, an engagement is almost the same as being married. We were together 3 ½ years, when the only way I could find out of the verbally abusive relationship was to just up and leave the church. I took the repercussions from the elders thirstily, anything to get out.

During that marriage, I rediscovered alcohol. I drank once in middle school while I was living with my grandmother, pouring gin into grape kool aid, just to see what my father had been so drawn towards. It also happened to be on a church night, and when I arrived, my friend Lonnie walked straight to me and asked if I had been drinking. I giggled and denied it. He told me to go park my butt down in a seat, immediately, passing me a piece of gum. The next time I drank was when I was in 10th grade, at an overnight with Shelley. We had warm Budweisers, which tasted like I imagined cat pee would. A neighborhood boy found me laying in the grass, my head spinning. I didn't like how I felt, out of control, and vowed to never drink again.

But there were weddings and dinners, and friends over, and now I felt that drinking made me fun. I loved dancing but was always embarrassed by my lack of skills. Alcohol made me feel like a disco queen. I was more open to the raunchy ideas my husband had, and I thought if I would just concede to them, he would pay more attention to me and stop treating me like the 20-year-old I was.

I drank because I wanted to hide who I thought I was: prude, quiet, reserved, and no fun. Drinking, and subsequently cocaine, brought out the fun side of me, or so I thought.

When Jason told me that he and his father didn't think I could handle moving to Peru, I lost trust in myself again. If I wasn't able to move to Peru for a year, then I mustn't be able to do anything. I'm a failure. I failed my husband, and even his father didn't think I could do it. All the things I had accomplished to that day, faded into nothingness. Once again, the one person who I thought believed in me, actually didn't believe in me.

Back to cocaine and drinking I turned, two things I was good at, and didn't have to face the apparently stick in the mud, anxious, immature person I was. I could be fun and happy and bouncy. I could out drink anyone at the bar, and consume an entire 8-ball by myself, and still go to work the next day and do a damn good job, by the way. Being drunk and high, I didn't have to admit to myself that I was scared of my own power, the substances gave me power. Without them, I was misdirected, unfocused and afraid. With them, all I had to do was dance, and out drink, and I was the star of the show. Obviously, everyone else knows better than me, so why should I trust myself when I think I can do something?

I now know, I am powerful and strong, brave and smart. I'm sensitive and intuitive, outspoken when needed and an ally. I don't have to wear anyone's persona but my own, and it's good enough even when I am afraid. I am the director, producer and writer of my own story.

I outlived two friends who struggled with addiction, out of sheer willpower. I raised two children, well, out of desire to give them what I didn't have. I persisted in a marriage for 20 years that didn't recognize my strengths, out of perseverance for doing what I believed was the right thing at the right time.

And if anyone ever tells me again, that I can't do something, I will use my words, my powerful strong words, and say,

"I will prove you wrong".

~ 25 ~

SHATTERED/MALIBU NIGHTS | 2021

Loss is nothing else but change, and change is Nature's delight.
~Marcus Aurelius

The grief hit me like a tsunami.

Seemingly out of nowhere, the bottom fell out, and I was enrobed in darkness like I'd never even dreamt of before. My heart pounded in my chest, my breath was shallow. I had a knot beneath my ribs the size of a grapefruit, and my whole body felt both numb and on fire. This was unlike any panic attack I had ever experienced, and then the sobs erupted from deep within my chest.

He had gone on two dates with her so far, and this being the third, I knew this was the end of the line for us.

I was frantic. Pacing in my apartment, I ran through my toolbox of calming techniques: deep breathing, shaking, moving. Nothing was working. I couldn't move enough to burn off the turmoil building inside. What did this mean for us going forward? Would she and I get along? Would she be good to my kids? Would she be good to him? Would he forget about me? Would he now only remember the bad times we had, and forget about our good times? Would we still be able to be friends? Would I never get to hug him again? The thought of him being intimate with her made my stomach lurch and my head dizzy.

This was it. We're done. There's no chance of reconciliation, ever again.

My house. My things. My bed. My kids. My love. My friend. Poof.

Wave after wave after wave crashed over me. I'll never get over this. I'll never be able to handle this. Why her? Why was it so easy for him to clean the house for her, and not me? Why all the effort for her? Why the dates with her that were spent out all day, when our time together was Netflix, every single evening? How is it so easy for him to get over me, and I'm here feeling like I'm being crushed by a boulder?

You're shit. You're fat. You're old. You think too much. You should have never left. Why didn't you just keep your big fat mouth shut? Why didn't you just ignore everything? You'll never find anyone again. All the men your age are so gross, and the ones that aren't, are definitely not interested in *you*. Your kids are going to forget about you. They're going to love her more. You're just going to be a distant memory for everyone, especially him. You'll be nothing but a blip on his radar, a bad memory that he's glad to leave in the rearview.

If someone or something could have ripped my heart from my chest, I would have gladly accepted that over what I was feeling.

God, please make this feeling go away. Just let me be at peace. PLEASE. The pleading turned to anger. "Why am I even asking YOU for anything? Why would you answer me now? You didn't hear me the whole marriage, when I did everything you asked of me. I did the best I could, I tried, and you know it. If marriage is so sacred to you, why couldn't you have saved this one?" It was pointless to plead or be angry with God, because he wasn't there. And why would I expect him to be? Was he there when my mother in law died? Was he there when her marriage broke up? Was he there when little children were dying of cancer? I was sick of bargaining with him. I'm just supposed to wait until heaven to be happy, while Doug gets his happily ever after now? When everything has come so easy to him, and I've had to struggle? Fuck you, God. Fuck. You.

Your kids are better off without you. You know you can't handle this pain on your own. You know you're never going to get past this. Just leave your kids, so they don't have to deal with your shit anymore. No one here wants to deal with your shit. You're too complicated, too emotional. Why can't you just sit quiet and shut up??

Remembering an Investigation Discovery episode I had seen where the wife poisoned her husband with antifreeze, I decided that's what I was going to do. Just get through tonight, and then go to the store. It's supposed to taste like Gatorade anyway, so no big deal.

Putting a gun to my head was the best option, but it would be too messy. I didn't want my kids to see my head blown off, and leave them with that memory. Unless I could aim the gun at my throat and hit the medulla, then maybe my brains wouldn't be all over the apartment.

I called my best friend and asked her if she would come stay the night with me. If I could just get to the morning, I could go get the antifreeze and die on my terms, with little mess. She scoffed at me, telling me that I shouldn't allow him to bother me. Of course, that makes sense logically, but I wasn't hearing it. I scrolled through my phone, looking for someone, anyone, that I could reach out to, but there was no one I felt safe enough to confide in. I finally reached out to a friend on Facebook, telling her I was done with this life. She understood, and said she respected my decision. That was a relief. Why do we force people to stay in places where they don't want to be anymore? Why are the feelings of the living more important than the ones who have to deal with the pain? She asked if I would first consider watching a couple TikTok videos that talked about soul contracts, and how if I left now, I would have to come back and do it again, potentially with a worse life. At that point in time, coming back as a cockroach felt like a much better life than feeling this heartbreak.

I made it to the next morning, exhausted. Doug and I were supposed to see each other, and I held onto the hope that maybe the shine had worn off, and they decided to no longer see each other. It wasn't the case. He was unsure of the direction it was going, but he was still very much interested in her. I pled my case once more, asking to get back together. He said he would think about it, and that was enough to tide me over.

The next day was Monday. I didn't text him all day, until after work. He told me he was going to meet her for dinner to see where they stood, because at least I was showing interest in him. I was hopeful and doubtful all at once, and once again, the wind was knocked out of my sails when he sent a text that read, "I guess I'll give it 2-3 months and see what happens." Fuck. Another night of sobbing, pleading with whoever lived in the sky, and my world was dark once again.

When I woke again, I found my gun. Drinking antifreeze would take 12-24 hours to kill me, and even then, Google wasn't clear on how much it would take. With my luck, I would end up permanently damaging my kidneys, and end up in the psych ward. I would rather be dead than to be in the hospital. I flipped open the barrel, and it was empty. The fuck??? Where were my bullets? I always kept my gun loaded. I scoured the apartment, searching for them. My boss texted me about work, and I replied back with, "Do you have time to meet with me today?"

I sat down in his office, and closed the door. He looked at me, apprehensive.

"I just...I just didn't realize how much my divorce was affecting me until my daughter graduated, and then we wrapped up the golf tournament. I came home afterwards, and I was just...alone, nothing to do. I was keeping busy, and didn't realize how depressed I am."

"What can we do to help?"

"Can you please make a call to my GP and get me in today?"

"Today?"

"Now."

He got up from his desk, and out the door. A few minutes later, he came back, and said I had an appointment at 1:30.

"I think I need a few days off to go see my mom. Can I use my PTO?"

"Absolutely. And if you need more than what you've accrued, take whatever time you need."

"Thank you. So much."

As soon as I had the prescription in my hand, I swallowed the pills, dry. I texted my brother, telling him I was driving down to visit, but I didn't want to see anyone but him and my parents. Intuitively, he immediately called me.

"I was waiting for this. I knew as soon as Anabel graduated, this was going to come. I'll see you tomorrow. I love you."

I spent the next three days at my parents' house. When I walked in their door late Wednesday night, I told them, "I think I'm having a nervous breakdown." My Dad jumped out of his recliner and wrapped me in a huge hug. When I left on Saturday, I thought I was better. I spent the drive home in complete silence, driving the eight hour trip straight through. It was peppered with outbursts at the God I so believed in for so many years, tears, and soothing words to myself. I condemned and praised God, talked to myself as if I were my own mother, and drove, numb.

I felt like a zombie, disconnected from reality. It was all I could do to make myself eat once a day. I would get up, go to work, come home, lay on the couch, force-feed myself, go to sleep, and repeat.

On Tuesday, I got the news that Doug and his new girl would be taking a trip out of the country. My son let it slip, because Doug was too chicken shit to tell me himself. I wanted to believe the best in him, telling myself that he hadn't yet told me because he didn't want to hurt me, but I had been telling myself stories about him for twenty years: that he meant well, he was misguided, had a bad childhood, was scared and insecure. But my heart was crushed. I wanted to take an exotic trip with him. I wanted day-long dates with him. I missed our early dating days, that had been so sweet, and were buried under the day-to-day bullshit.

I take down from the refrigerator the picture of us in Destin. We are both tan and smiling, getting ready to take a sunset boat ride. I set it on my coffee table, and in front of it, I place a pink candle, surrounded by dried rose petals, rose quartz, and black tourmaline. I light the candle, and speak to the picture.

"I remember matching with you, and being enamored with your kind, brown eyes. We weren't able to meet for a few weeks since I was still in Florida, so I would look at your profile pictures often, taking in every detail. I memorized your smile, your hands, your legs, your arms, your shoulders. I was so nervous when we met, because you seemed too good to be true, and I didn't want to be let down. I kept you at arm's length until I couldn't anymore. Laying in bed with you, talking until late at night, I watched your mouth, how it moved, how your tongue formed words. I swore I could see into your soul through your eyes, and I imagined the little boy you once were. Wrapping me in your arms in a hug immediately calmed me, and still does to this day. I loved how your hand fit in mine, and how smooth your skin was. I loved kissing you, and loving you, laughing with you. I loved nuzzling the crook of your neck, and feeling your arm muscles when they flexed. I wasn't going to let myself fall for anyone so soon, but I did. I adored every part of you, and craved your stable nature. Knowing you made me believe there was a God, and he was good. Finally, finally, you were here. All the shit I had dealt with up til now was finally being wiped off my slate.

Then, gradually, we became codependent, and eventually, toxic. Through all our rough days, I held in my heart the little boy I saw, hoping that loving him would heal us. I prayed multiple times a day to just make me quieter and calmer. To be the peace we both desperately needed. But in so doing, I felt like I was abandoning myself more and more, and we became more and more distant. It eventually felt like the chasm was so vast that there was no way to repair it but to burn it and start over.

Asking you to go to therapy wasn't because I felt like there was something wrong with you. To the contrary, it was because I knew how amazing you are, that I wanted you to break down that wall you have around your emotions. I realized how tough the wall was when your mom passed away, and you couldn't cry; but that little boy stared up at me, pleading with me, to step to the stage and speak about her.

I've never not loved you. I've never given up on you. Leaving wasn't giving up, it was an attempt at a reset, that backfired.

My wish is that you find someone who sees all the things that are beautiful about you. Maybe one day it'll be me again, but if it's not, just know that I do love you, immensely. And anyone who breaks your heart again, will have me to reckon with. Just please, be cautious."

The candle burned for over 8 hours, and by the time it went out, I had reached the meaning of "Malibu Nights": I've tried all I can to rekindle the relationship, now all that's left to do is be sad, and wait for time to heal my shattered heart. I had to speak those words to him in order to survive our breakup and forge a new path.

26

TRUST AND BELIEVE, PART TWO
| 2022

God has entrusted me with myself.
~Epictetus

As much as what my father did to me impacted me, it was almost as if it was expected. I knew he was a drunk and unreliable, and while I hoped he would eventually get better, I didn't hold much faith in it. We had been through the same thing over and over again, AA, the hospital, the women's shelters. I was frustrated with my mother for not being able to see what I saw, and couldn't understand why he was still around.

But what pulled the rug out from underneath me was when DFACS was brought into the situation, and my mother was given a choice. Not knowing that bit of information, I just automatically assumed that now my father would be removed from the home, and the three of us could heal finally. A week went by, and I was shuffled between my cousin, my great aunt, and my grandmother's homes. I was assigned case workers, group and individual counseling, and appointments were made for my testimony and the validity of my virginity. I was called down to the front office at school almost weekly for yet another appointment, no one preparing me for any of them. They were just random. I never knew who would be picking me up, but it was typically my Guardian ad Litem, Barbara.

After a week, I realized I wasn't going home just yet, but I believed it would be soon. After the meeting one evening, I asked my grandmother to take me to my house to pick up some things. She did. When we pulled into the driveway, I reached for the door handle to get out and go in the house. She stopped me, and told me she had to be the one to go in. I couldn't. I sat stunned for a second, and asked why. She told me that I just wasn't allowed to go inside. My own house.

Then it hit me like a ton of bricks. HE was there.

I jumped out of the car anyway, and ran up to the back door, trying the handle. It was locked. I banged on the frame, "Mom! Mom, answer the door!" She came to the door, sheepishly, and squeezed her way outside. "Why can't I go in? Is he here?? Why is *he* here?"

"It's complicated," she replied flatly.

"You picked *him* over *me*?!" I yelled, the rage building inside me. "I need my stuff! Let me go get my stuff!"

(And this, my friends, is why my things are so important to me. Why I keep precious items in a plastic bin, just in case I need to grab them and go)

"Tell me what you need, and I'll go get it for you. But you can't go inside." Her voice showed no emotion, no empathy.

"Why is he in there?! Why is he still here?!" I was simmering. My eyes were burning with hot tears, my stomach was balled in fury. My heart was crushed, but she was meeting me with such apathy, that I refused to let her see. I wanted to pour gasoline on the house, light a match, and walk away.

I pushed her aside, grabbed the door, and shoved my way into the house. I heard scuffling. I can't remember if my brother was home, but it's likely he was, or I probably would have set the house on fire. I walked straight into my room, and saw that someone, probably my father, had been sleeping in my bed. My mother always made the bed, and my father didn't.

"*Stay out of my bed!!*" I yelled, yanking dresser drawers open, not even knowing what to grab. My mother had come into the house, and stood in the doorway of my room, saying nothing. "I HATE YOU!" I screamed. She appeared unphased. I shoved past her once again, leaving the back door open, and got into my grandmother's car. "Let's just go," I told her, and we drove away.

For the next 12 years, my mother and I played a game with no name. My role was to stuff my anger and hurt towards her because she refused to address it. We co-existed once I moved back home that August, until I eventually moved out. We would have occasional arguments, where I would either explode in anger, or would passive-aggressively defy her. In either case, she showed no emotion. In one instance, she was getting onto me about something while I was washing dishes. I turned to face her, with a glass in my hand. I looked her dead in the eye, and released the glass, shattering it on the Terrazzo floor. She snickered and walked away.

Any time I would reach out to her for comfort, she was flat. She could occasionally say some of the right words, but they were vapid.

When my niece was born, a common ground was fostered. We connected over our mutual adoration of this gorgeous, brown-eyed child. I began to hope that we could finally mend our relationship. I wrote her a heartfelt letter, asking her if we could talk about those last four years we lived together. She never replied. After a few weeks, I called her to ask if she had received it. She had, and I asked if we could talk about it.

"You can't blame everyone else for your problems. I can't do anything about the past."

I sat with that answer for a few days.

I could force the issue, but knowing her, it would do no good. I could cut her off completely, but that would lessen my opportunities to see my niece. My mother would be unaffected by this choice anyway. Or I could burn the idea that she was capable of ever being the mother I hoped to have. I could create a new box for her: one where she is my mother by birth, but not by heart. She would be a friend that I kept at arm's length, but one that couldn't be trusted with things of importance. I had to recognize that I would never get the reaction or response from her that I so desperately craved. If it's not in her best interest, it doesn't happen. She doesn't think she needs deep connection, or maybe she's afraid to pursue it.

Maybe she was hurt so badly that she closed herself off completely.

It's only recently that I see the correlation between my mother and Doug. In essence, I married my mother. Their stories are quite different, but their behaviors are identical. They more than likely have been hurt so deeply in their past somewhere, that they choose to manipulate instead of being raw to get what they want and need. They choose safety and comfort over risk. They see feelings of any sort, beyond what they consider love, to be weakness. They numb, whether it be with alcohol or monkey barring into relationships, rather than face hard truths and healing.

It's partially why I was so drawn to Doug...seeing something inside him that needed to be healed and loved. I still to this day see the little boy I envision being hurt so badly somehow, and desperate for someone to recognize that. But like my mother, he doesn't want to address it. They both want just the unconditional love, without the pain of understanding why they need it. I can only speculate what either of them experienced. My mother, possibly the trauma of religion and never being able to meet the standards of my grandmother; and then the extreme trauma experienced at my father's hands. Doug, also religious trauma, and what I'm sure was emotional and physical abuse by his father. And it goes back generations. My father saw his mother murdered, and then consequently the experience of war, which introduced him to drugs.

I, on the other hand, have also experienced trauma, but display it in other ways. Not wanting anyone to ever feel disappointment, betrayal, or hurt, I soothe, gloss over, and conform to others' needs and wants (i.e. people pleasing/self-sacrificing). Some people soothe their trauma by taking, others soothe it by giving. Neither way is better than another, because both ways are manipulation tactics to avoid inner work.

So how do you "get" someone to see you? You can't. You can only choose how to interact with them further. I had to acknowledge that my mother wasn't capable of loving me the way I desired, and choose to create an entirely different way to be with her. With Doug, should we ever explore our relationship again, I'll have to learn to see myself, believe in my own value, be my own hype man. I'll have to recognize when he's being manipulative, because it's his way of self-soothing, and be strong enough to not allow myself to be guilted into things I don't want to do, just to garner his approval.

The Universe provides us with people for our souls to learn lessons. It's a self-guided class, but there's no escaping it. It's my belief that my relationship with Jason was to show me what I'm capable of, that I can be loved exactly where I am, and that unconditional love exists. There's always strings attached to any relationship you're in, but some strings are longer or looser than others. The strings with Jason were elastic, the strings with my mother and Doug were more rigid. It's just part of the lesson.

I don't know the purpose or lesson with my relationship with my mother, except maybe to just love her; but I do know my relationship with Doug was to recognize and potentially heal the damage caused by my relationship with my mother. It just took me a long time to learn it: I have to value myself first, before I can expect anyone else to value me. And in that valuing myself, I can decide what's acceptable and what's not.

I have to trust and believe in me, first.

27

COMING TO THE TABLE | 2020

Be who you were created to be, and you will set the world on fire.
~St. Catherine of Siena

Remember as a kid, when your family would have big gatherings, and the adults would sit at one table, and the kids would sit at another? The kids' table was definitely more fun, but the adults' table always looked so enticing.

When we're in a relationship with someone who just can't or won't do the work needed to keep the relationship functioning at optimum level, it's frustrating and sometimes scary. You're eating the same meal, but sitting at two different tables. At the kids' table, it doesn't matter if you have your elbows on it, or spill your drink, or make fart jokes. But at the adults' table, you're expected to mind your manners, eat politely, and carry on conversation. Some people just don't ever want to leave the kids' table.

We hear this phrase a lot when it comes to relationships: what do you bring to the table? Most answers are common: good job, stability, loyalty. That's the meal. But what differentiates what table you actually get assigned to are the nuanced items: empathy, ability to grow, maturity, open-mindedness, support, trust (and trust is even more nuanced in and of itself...more on that later).

Conflict in our relationships can be one way to determine who is sitting at which table. When conflict arises, how is it handled? Are your needs and requests ignored, shot down, or somehow negated? Do we avoid it because it hasn't gone well in the past?

We tend to move away from conflict, or move towards it, thinking that fighting harder is the solution. It's uncomfortable either way, but both parties have to be in a space where you're willing to embrace the discomfort and face your own discomfort with being uncomfortable. Why would you rather just check out or pretend that something didn't happen, or even worse, settle for the situation you're in? So many of us are stuck in relationships where we're unwilling or unable to have the conflict needed to bring resolution that potentially bring us closer. We settle for partial connection, because no connection is scarier.

There's a few reasons for that. Typically we get stuck in a cycle of thinking that if we speak up, things will go poorly, and the other person will be upset with us, or leave us. Or we minimize the issues, telling ourselves it's not that big of a deal. Ultimately, this is a form of self-gaslighting. We aren't honoring ourselves and our individual wants and needs for fear of taking away someone else's wants and needs. We eat our own discomfort to "save" others from feeling discomfort. We can speak up and lose the relationship with the other person, or we can keep silent, and lose the relationship with our truest self. Neither of these options feel really good, I can promise you that.

I saw a post on Facebook today that read: "A man [or woman] will never grow up if the people around them always justify their behavior."

In essence, when we avoid conflict so someone else doesn't have to be unsettled, we are justifying, condoning, and permitting their behavior. If we allow ourselves to shrink for fear of upsetting someone, we are telling them that how they're behaving is okay with us. Letting it go on long enough, it then becomes our fault. We are betraying ourselves, and sacrificing ourselves, for another's comfort. I'm guilty of this in more than one relationship. Not wanting to hold my ex-husband back from his dreams, I kept silent until the discomfort grew out of control, and I acted out. I was more concerned with their comfort, than trying to find a compromise so that we could both be comfortable and content. And creating destruction in the wake.

Maybe you're in a situation where you have spoken up, embraced the conflict, spoke your truth, and it just went nowhere. It's defeating, and it just seems easier to change the channel. Why do we choose to be in relationships with people who are choosing to not sit at our table? Why do we beg them to just come over and sit at the adults' table, when they're perfectly content at the kids' table? Sometimes we just don't know any better. Sometimes we just don't know that this isn't the norm. There are other possibilities.

We hear about the power of single person being able to affect change in a relationship. But we also have to come to terms that if the other person isn't willing to come sit at the table where you are, you're limited. Even if you got up and dragged them to the adults' table, they're going to keep fighting to go back to the kids' table. They're going to keep putting their elbows on the table, spilling their drinks, and making fart jokes. They want to be with the kids. Not everyone wants to sit at the adults' table.

We can't point the finger at them, calling them immature for wanting to stay there. It can be uncomfortable changing tables. You have to learn new rules, new language, new manners. Imagine moving to a new country and not being able to speak the language or know their customs. If you went there willingly, of course you would want to do your best to learn, but it would still take some time. If you were forced to move there, you would more than likely complain about it, wishing you could move back to your former country. You might even be a jerk about it and refuse to learn the language and the customs and just do your own thing ('Merica!).

Maybe you've asked them to come to the table in all the right ways, pointing out how great the conversation is, informing them of all the new things they'll be talking about with the adults. Still, they refuse. Or they come, thinking they're ready to sit with the grown people, but they bring all their sloppy manners and inappropriate jokes, making everyone around them uncomfortable. You could leave the table with them, and find a table of your own, leaving your friends and family; or you could send them back to their own table, and let them enjoy where they are.

Not wanting to argue in front of the kids or risk not being able to see them every day, I kept silent with Doug until I made myself physically ill. I left the table where I was sitting, and sat with him, all by ourselves. I missed the conversations I had with my friends and family. I ate at a completely different restaurant, because he didn't want to join.

~ 28 ~

SOUL CRUSHING | 2020

To be yourself in a world that is constantly trying to make you some-
thing
else is the greatest accomplishment.
~Ralph Waldo Emerson

In our last session with Ed, who we've been working with since June or July, I tell him, "I'm not coming home unless you go to counseling for yourself". He declines, stating that he has nothing he needs to work on, that he's happy with himself, and he's not going to change. Emboldened, angry and hurt, I tell him that's the only way I am coming home. He stands his ground.

I had driven to Florida at the beginning of August to clear my head and decide what exactly it was I needed from the marriage to make it work.

The next morning, I pack my things and drive back to Georgia. I move my things from the car into my office. He is surprised that I mean it when I say I'm not coming home.

He tells women he meets on dating apps that I told him I just wanted to be single, but what he doesn't realize is that is the result

106

of this failed relationship. I feel as if I'm dying, whether I stay or I go, so I may as well go. What example am I setting for my daughter if I stay in a relationship where only one person is getting what they need? What am I telling her, and myself for that matter, about my worth? I'm only underlining that my use and purpose here is to serve others. And while that is our purpose on some level, it's not our sole purpose, and especially not to the detriment of our own health.

He tells them that I didn't put the relationship first, that I didn't make our marriage a priority, that I refused to compromise. When I find these things out, my head swims. What then, was it I was doing all these 20 years? If I wasn't compromising, or putting the marriage first, or being devoted, what would it be called?

My very soul feels crushed. My entire life, I have stepped aside, quieted down, watered down, backed down, tiptoed around, to accommodate everyone else. I've tried so hard not to play the victim card, but at this moment, it feels like that's all I've been. A people-pleaser. Feeling that I'm too much or not enough, but never just right. Feeling that there's something so inherently wrong with me that I cannot be loved for who I am. And who am I, anyway?

My father: you want to drink, then drink. You want to yell at me, spank me, so be it. But don't touch my mother or brother.

My mother: you want to abide by your religious beliefs, that's ok. But you can't force them on everyone, no matter how convinced you are that they're truth.

My grandmother: you grew up in an era where girls and women were second place. And yet, after your death, I see where you were rebellious and stood up for yourself. Why wasn't that allowed for anyone else?

Jason: I stepped aside from our relationship because I felt like I was holding you back. Who was I to keep you from traveling the world?

Doug: Only until your drama seeped over onto me, did I speak up. You put so much emphasis on the relationship being the most important, but it doesn't seem to matter to you the health of the individuals inside the relationship. As long as you're content, it matters not how someone else feels. I cleaned my side of the street before I entered a relationship with you, but you came to the door, arms full, and handed it to me. A team carries them together, they don't just dump them on someone else and watch as they struggle. And then you drag my name through the mud, saying I'm the one who isn't devoted. You've played enough sports to know that one person can't carry the whole team. You're like JR Smith, every time I went to pass the ball to you, you either weren't there, or you went the wrong direction.

Am I angry with you? Yes, in some ways. I feel betrayed, un-important. I feel like I was used for your needs alone, with little in return. I'm also angry at myself. For believing that I had found someone who would truly love me for me, for believing the fairy tale, for thinking you knew better on how to be better. What's better for you isn't better for everyone, and that's the problem when we think we know better. We need to allow people to be themselves, and work around that. And if we can't deal with how they are, let them go. No threats to take away their children, or their life. No manipulation on how difficult your life will be. Let people be who they are, and stop trying to hammer them into your molds.

~ 29 ~

A LLAMAR AL PAN PAN, Y AL VINO VINO

"To call the bread bread, and to call the wine wine." ~Spanish idiom

"To fight unhappiness, one must first expose it.:" ~Simone de Beauvoir

Abuse is such a strong word that it can seem overly dramatic to use. We want to save the impact of the word for extreme situations, and understandably so. The frequency of using the term can seem to lessen the severity of it.

When it comes to emotional abuse (which I instead call manipulation, due to fear of ramifications), what can happen is that your tolerance for it will increase over time and you will become more immune to substandard behavior. When you are in this space, emotional manipulation can become more ubiquitous, but you won't notice the gravity of it because "that's the way it's always been", or "they didn't really mean it that way". You begin to question yourself: maybe you're just too sensitive, or reading into things. You make excuses.

What's likely is that it wasn't always that way. Early on in the relationship, you were probably quite happy. You were both meeting each other's needs and supportive of each other. Slowly, some of the manipulator's selfish behavior began, and you started to intuit that things were different. Situations begin to support them and their needs more than yours.

When emotional manipulation begins to surface, blame is shifted to the emotionally manipulated partner so that the manipulator doesn't have to take responsibility. On top of that, the manipulator consistently finds an excuse or explanation for their bad behavior. No matter how wrong the manipulator is, they'll find a way to make themselves right. You can't figure out how they do it (Logic Magic, as I like to call it), but emotional manipulators find innovative methods to make their partner see them as innocent, naive, ignorant of their own behavior, and possibly a victim of the circumstances. A manipulator's rationality can often be illogical but worded in a way that sounds wise and sensible.

On the outside looking in, I was amazed at how deftly Doug was able to turn the tables away from him and back to me. It was never his fault, it was always me who was taking things the wrong way, misunderstanding things, too reactionary, or just being too sensitive. Later on, he actually told me that I shouldn't have "let" him manipulate me.

Manipulators are great at playing naïve when you know they aren't. They're actually quite intelligent, which is how they got so good at wordplay and deception in the first place. If you see "obtuse" behavior when all other times they are intelligent and rational, it could be a manipulation tactic. Is this learned behavior, or is it a defense mechanism? The jury is still out.

To me, marriage isn't about always being together and doing everything together, we are not one and the same person. I have different ideals, interests & personality. But I felt like I couldn't ever leave his side to be who I wanted to be, do things I wanted to do, without feeling like I was neglecting Doug.

Probably I should have been more outspoken but after a while of doing it, it felt pointless. Everything I ever brought up was always excused with logic and trying to make things easier for him. I think deep down he somewhat agreed with me, and I think that's why he was so quick to buy things for me: to make up for that guilt.

I tried to just wait it out and see if things would change. But as I waited it out, I got more and more resentful. And I wasn't sure how to make that go away. I should have just taken the chance and kept running my mouth and just said what I felt, but that still wouldn't have made any difference. He still would not have made any changes, or at the very least, seen my point of view.

Don't get me wrong, eventually I got complacent too. I bought into consumerism when I knew that wasn't who I was. I made my kids consumers, knowing that wasn't the kind of people I wanted to raise. I got caught up in Doug's and his family's ideals and values. In my soul, they are not my values, but I sacrificed them and gave them up because it felt easier at the time. I kept thinking that at some point, I would be able to be myself in the marriage if I just gave in a little. I spent time and energy on him so he could have what he deemed to be peace. I was the "strong one", so I could deal with it.

I thought if I put my time in, proved my worth to him, that I would be freer to do the things I need to do, but I still felt obligated to "babysit" him and make sure he was pacified. I watered down my personality to make it more digestible. I quit visiting my family because I didn't want to make him feel neglected...and I didn't want my family to see how conflicted I felt. I was embarrassed that I was allowing someone to dictate my actions and control me. I followed along with who he was and what he liked, saying yes when I wanted to say no, not standing my ground on my opinions, second guessing myself in an attempt to appease him.

The second guessing was the worst part. I quit trusting my own judgement. I became afraid of myself and my own choices, to the extent that I couldn't even make a decision on what clothes to wear, or if I should leave the house. I stopped answering my phone when my Gramma would call for fear that she would be able to tell I was fading away.

For most of our marriage, the research and introspection was on how I could fix the marriage, what could I do more or better? I'm not perfect, I'll be the first to admit it. I was more than willing to make sure this relationship was different than the others I had previously. But it was a matter of months before I started to see that I was left unprotected by him, and not "allowed" to stand up for myself. Time after time, I was told to just ignore things said by his family and ex-wife.

Just let it go.

Just ignore it.

Why can't you be the bigger person?

Why can't you just keep the peace?

I had opened my heart, and repeatedly, it was pricked.

I was constantly told how I'm too much a guy and not a girly girl, but at the same time, I'm supposed to toughen up under ridicule and not be so sensitive. Which is it? You can't keep poking a wound and expect it to heal. You can't expect repeated friction not to cause a callous.

Maybe I am an overly sensitive person, but I believe sensitivity is a gift. I know for sure it's what my friends and family love about me. It surprises me so much lately when I am called kind, considerate, sweet, loving, or a sensitive soul. Because I don't feel like it. I feel bitter, angry, resentful. I felt like a bull in a China shop, an unfettered sail flapping in the wind. I don't remember the happy-go-lucky, free spirit I used to be. She doesn't exist. My face is a constant frown, my body feels heavy and tired.

It comes down to trust. At the very core of our issues, it's trust. Not that I don't trust him to be faithful, but I don't trust him with my heart, my feelings. Every time I approached him with concerns that had hurt my heart, I was met with resistance and dismissal. Every time I was a GIRL, I was essentially told to "man up". And then conversely, I was told I was too bossy and controlling. Every. Single. Time I shared my thoughts or feelings, I was scoffed at.

It's no wonder I had no idea which way is up.

~ 30 ~

REBOS IS SOBER SPELLED BACKWARDS

One day at a time.
~Alcoholics Anonymous

My brother and I run through the halls of Church By The Sea, chasing each other, opening doors to classrooms, pretending the church is haunted. It smells less like the Kingdom Hall, and more like an elementary school, minus the canned peas scent from the school cafeteria. The classrooms have chalkboards that we draw on, and paper and crayons that we color with. The excitement for fear of getting lost, and opening doors to dark rooms is intoxicating to me.

We sit in the waiting room of the house turned AA meeting facility, smoke-filled air, and the odor of coffee hanging heavy. It's called The REBOS Club. I have no idea what the name means at the time, but I like going there. We go as a family sometimes, and it's one of the rare times we do anything together as a family. The smoke smell doesn't bother me, because our father smokes in the house, but with nearly everyone smoking, the air is cloudy. The

114

people that walk in and out are friendly, and greet us, and our father loves introducing us as his kids. When he's trying, he really tries, and I like that he seems proud of us.

We wander the courtyard of Sacred Heart Catholic Church, dense with trees dripping with Spanish moss. The covered sidewalks weave all over the campus, and we explore. The meetings we attend are always in the evenings, and being outside as the sun turns dark, turns the church campus into a wooded forest with wolves and creatures of the night lurking around every corner.

AA and Al-Anon are in our DNA. Our father has been attending meetings since he moved to Florida, whether ordered by the courts, my mom, or his own desire to get better, I don't know. I am thankful for the naivete bestowed upon me by my mother, because had I known what was really going on at that time, I may have been demolished emotionally. At this age, everything is an adventure, and I am fairly oblivious to my homelife.

Our father lands a stint at St. Anthony's Hospital, and I childishly think it's because of his back pain. When we visit him, we get free Sprites, and sometimes candy or snacks from the vending machine. I've come to love the hospital coffee, with the powdered creamer and murky flavor. It's much later in life that I find out he was really in the hospital for his heroin addiction. Suddenly, the rings he made from the handles of spoons make sense.

I find myself in my first NA meeting in 1995, off Haines Road. I walk into the familiar scene, and find my seat. The coffee is still awful, so I pass it by. I've only been doing cocaine for about 6 months, but I know that I'm hiding it, and that's not a good sign. Just as the meeting is about to begin, a familiar face walks in with a guy. I scroll through the index file in my brain, trying to place who she is. After 30 minutes of sneaking glances her way, it dawns on me. It's Jenny, from the Kingdom Hall. Perfect, gorgeous, uber popular Jenny. The one who tormented me all through middle school and part of high school, until she got pregnant and had other things to do. I'm aghast. She's not so perfect after all. After the meeting ends, I leave, and vow to never go back to meetings again, because now it's my chance to better myself.

When I'm in a relationship, I'm addicted to alcohol, drugs, coffee, food, placating others' feelings, controlling situations, keeping up the appearances of myself and those around me, being complicit in lies, church, being a wretched sinner, endless social media scrolling, and making sure everyone is happy.

When I'm on my own, I'm addicted to sunsets, rainbows, morning and evening meditations, long showers, shaving my legs, painting my toes, making my bed, the smell of flowers blooming, the slight change in the air when the weather changes, the sound of the ocean, tipping my face towards the sun, blasting music with the windows rolled down, complimenting random strangers, babies, writing, giving away money, and books.

It's ironic, the differences. What is it about relationships that makes people like me feel the need to lose themselves? What is it about relationships that makes people like me find toxic substances to use instead of the lovely things when we're not in a relationship? Do we feel less than when with someone else? Do we we're feel too much when with someone else?

I wish I knew the answer.

~ 31 ~

I WENT TO SLEEP | 2019

It is not up to you to finish the task, but you are not free to avoid it.
~Pirkei Avot

I read the Marianne Williamson books, I listened to her CDs, often. I knew that my sensitivity was important I knew that there was something to be changed, but nothing was changing.

Thinking maybe I was just crazy and making a big deal out of nothing and maybe Marianne really didn't know what she was talking about as well as all the other feminists who are attempting to make changes and open our eyes, I went to sleep. I went to sleep in devout Christianity. I went to sleep in patriarchy. I went to sleep in my comfortable bed of what I had grown up in. I went to sleep, trusting that those who had gone before me knew what they were doing and I could rest in that.

I'd wake up, groggily, and make a comment here and there about racism and the mistreatment of women, but when it fell on deaf ears and blind eyes, I quit. Maybe I'm being too radical. Maybe I'm not trusting in God enough. He'll fix it when he comes back. I stayed in my comfortable bed, waiting to be flown into the sky where utopia awaited. Isn't that what we're told to do? This life is just a waiting room for the next one. Let God handle it. We just trod along, making sure we don't screw up so we don't lose our Golden ticket.

My bed was comfortable, but my sleep was fitful. I constantly questioned myself and my parenting, my homemaking, my wife skills...because I couldn't risk screwing up and not being raptured with my children. I couldn't risk Doug taking my children. I was constantly frozen, second guessing my every move.

Until the sermon about Lot's daughters. And I knew that I had to wake up. I knew that I had to wake up for my daughter! And when I did, still nothing had changed. We were still fighting for equality. We're still fighting racism. We're still fighting for women's rights. We're still fighting the patriarchy. How long do we fight?

But I also knew that my sleeping through this was not going to make anything any better. Maybe waking up isn't going to change anything, but it will show my daughter that I care. That I care for her. That I care for her future. That I care for her friends. That I care for her rights. That I care for her children. That I care for her grandchildren. If I go back to sleep now, I am participating in the trampling of her future and all future generations. I am complicit in the things that are going on. Maybe my little pebble will not make any difference whatsoever, but maybe my little pebble well at least show her and her friends that I care. That there's someone out there who is listening. That there's someone out there who thinks that they are worth the fight. They are worth hearing, seeing, being listened to.

~ 32 ~

THIS AIN'T IT | 2020

The history of progress is written in the blood of men and women who have dared to espouse an unpopular cause, as, for instance, the black man's right to his body, or woman's right to her soul.
~Emma Goldman

When society, and more specifically, religion, teaches people from a very young age that they should choose their life's career path by eighteen, and that the person they marry should be the one they remain with for life, without offering the ability to explore who we are and what we like...

We set up a society that looks like it's floundering.

There are some religions out there that tell you that dating is for the sole purpose of marriage. That's an outdated and archaic belief, even more so now that women have more rights than they did in generations past. For millennia, marriage for women was a safety net, and often they had no choice in the matter. As recent as two generations ago, women married not just for love, but to be provided for, as it wasn't accepted for them to hold jobs, vote or even purchase their own home if they were even permitted to hold a job.

While the pressure isn't nearly as equal on men as it is on women, they do still feel a great responsibility. As mentioned above, once high school graduation was completed, it was expected to decide then and there where you would attend college and choose a career that you would remain in until retirement. Options were limited, and included being forcibly drafted into wars the common person had no idea what were being fought for.

We aren't provided much opportunity to decide "This Ain't It".

~ 33 ~

IT'S NOT YOU, IT'S ME | 2021

Heaven is under our feet as well as over our heads.
~Henry David Thoreau

As I proofread through the first few thousand words I've written so far, one of the patterns I see is an almost compulsive need to give implicit credit to other people in my past for my bigger growth stages. It borders on obsessive reminiscing, and when I took a closer look at why, it became more clear.

It was because I wasn't willing to give credit to myself.

An acorn always has the power to become an oak tree. If it's planted in concrete, it's probably not going to grow. If it's planted in rocky soil with little nutrients, the growth will be stunted. But if it's planted in nice, loamy earth, with plenty of sunshine and water, its potential to grow is multiplied.

I was so eager to make sure I kept my place in line, that I even gave up credit for my own goddamn growth. It was impossible that it was merely the environment that dictated my growth or lack of. It *had* to be the person...

I did the same thing when I gave up cocaine. It couldn't possibly have been my own determination and willpower, it had to be an external celestial being who took credit.

The confines that I had grown up in kept me from seeing that I have the potential for full autonomy over my own life, growth, expansion, learning; or restriction.

My daughter, in her late high school years, was making choices that I didn't think were in her best interests. I didn't think that arbitrarily grounding her would help, so I discussed with her where the path she was heading could possibly lead, told her about situations I had gotten into when behaving as she was, and told her that she needed to sit down and figure out what was really at the bottom of why she was doing what she was doing. "I just like to party" wasn't a good enough answer, because WHY do you like to party? Are you trying to feel uninhibited? Do you think alcohol makes you more fun? Are you covering up other feelings? Her discipline was for her to journal what she was feeling and why.

I had so many people dictating how my life should be lived, that I didn't trust myself. I was always second guessing my choices, drawing out decisions for hours, days, weeks, months on end. I was always afraid of the consequences of shaming other people.

When I stepped into the relationship with Jason, there was little judgement, and so I could listen to my own thoughts. I could try on various experiences.

It wasn't the person that facilitated the journey, it was the environment.

My nephew once told me that people often lie because they are afraid to tell the truth. Your honest thoughts and answers aren't always wanted, so you lie about what you're thinking or feeling. Your line to walk is so narrow in certain families that if you step off even slightly, you're chastised for deviating from their plan, their way. So you lie about something you did while you weren't being watched. Most people are so convinced that their way is the absolute right way, that there's little room for trial and error.

Christianity, especially, claims to be the one true path, the tried and true way to live life, and they're so terrified of going to hell, that they forget that humans were given free will. It's that remembrance that we have free will that should expunge any repercussions of "shame" that might be brought on your image from another person acting out that free will.

Children "misbehaving" or going off on a path different than yours isn't a failure for your parenting skills. In fact, I would say that it makes you a better parent, because you didn't create a copy-paste of yourself and everyone in your small circle. The kids who march to a different beat are the innovators, the cycle breakers, the ones who elicit the change that is so very necessary and at the same time so frightening.

The only reason I sent my son off to military school was to evacuate him from the berating of his dad when he "screwed up".

It wasn't Jason the person who created the grounds for growth during our relationship. It was Jason the environment. It wasn't Jason who read the books, did the work, did the journaling, listened to my intuition, it was *me*. I could have easily remained as I was when I met him, and that would have been just fine, too. He would have loved me as an acorn, a seedling, or a sapling. It was *me* he loved, not my potential. The me and he that formed the we, was enough for him. My growth was mine to do, my free will to choose.

I'm grateful for the environment I was given with him, but ultimately...

I was the one who chose. I was the one who grew. I was the one who learned.

It's not you, it's actually... me.

~ 34 ~

MOVING GOALPOSTS | 2021

The emerging woman ... will be strong-minded, strong-hearted,
strongsouled,
and strong-bodied ... strength and beauty must go together.
~Louisa May Alcott

Numerous times during the end of my marriage, I was accused of constantly "moving the goalposts" in what I wanted from him in order to stay. At first glance, it seemed as if he was right. I really thought that if he offered to help more around the house, the issues we had would be gone. But the more I asked, or delegated things for him to assist with, I realized I was still exhausted. It was as much his house as mine, the kids were as much his as mine, and I couldn't understand why I needed to ask for the floor to be vacuumed, dinner to be made, or the kids driven somewhere. It became more obvious this was weaponized incompetence and inequitable division of labor. Even though he said he was willing to do what I asked, we were both adults, and it felt as if I was training another child.

Dishes laying in the sink only bothered him if the kids did it. The unvacuumed floor, and dusty surfaces were walked past without a second glance.

Once early on, I explained to him that an unkempt house reflected poorly on me, as the wife, mother and woman of the house. He brushed it off, saying that other people that came to visit should understand that we had kids and I wasn't at fault. Seemed logical enough. However, his thinking was also that if I drank too much, cussed or behaved in a way that wasn't of the utmost highest standards, reflected poorly on him. It took me decades to see the double standard. I was so busy trying to maintain perfection in his eyes, that I didn't see the forest for the trees.

I then moved the goalpost by telling him he needed to figure out what needed to be done around the house. "Make me a list and I'll do it," he responded. After 40 plus years of living, he still had to have a list made of basic household chores. I thought back to when we had dated, and he lived on his own, remembering that his toilet was dirty, his sheets hadn't been changed in months, and his house was overpowering with the smell of plug-ins. I had been so smitten with him, that I failed to see the conditions in which he had no problem living.

The goalpost was moved again when I asked for him to take initiative in our dates. "I don't know what there is to do around here," was his reply. Yet he could spend hours researching tires and rims for his car, or the best lifejacket for his jetski.

I moved it again by asking for him to "allow" me alone time. My need for downtime has nothing to do with my not wanting to be around my partner, it's a time for me to reset my internal system, just like rebooting a computer. Alone time isn't taking a shower, or with someone right there next to me, either, it's time for me to...be alone.

The final goalpost move was when I asked if it would be fine for me to create my podcast content, write this book, and post things on social media that may not align with his beliefs. You might wonder why I would even have to ask permission for such things, and you'd be right in your asking. I wasn't creating or posting highly controversial things, unless you are really so self-conscious that anything that is slightly in opposition to the image you want to portray causes you turmoil. See, being the bigger person or overlooking what someone else says only applied to me. I was the one who was supposed to overlook what his family said, I was the one who was supposed to be the bigger person and not take up for myself.

I'm forever grateful for the experience I had with Jason's family, because it showed me that it's possible to have differing, almost polarizing opinions, and you can still voice them and get along. No one in the family was ever told to go along just to get along. There were spirited, and sometimes heated, arguments. Sometimes people took breaks from each other for a time. But we all circled back around to loving and respecting each other.

Conversely, the window of individuality was so narrow, that Doug's family were practically clones of one another.

Midway through our marriage, my asks turned into complaints. I started to see how other husbands treated their wives and were equal partners in the marriage. Even women who stayed at home with the kids, had husbands who were more than willing to get up in the middle of the night, or cook dinner, or wash clothes. When I would ask for him to get up and get the babies, he would say he had to get up early for work, and that I could always nap during the day. When I couldn't or didn't nap, his response was that it wasn't his fault I didn't take advantage of the chance to do so. "Other women's husbands are probably out cheating on them, and you're upset that I'm playing video games? At least I'm home." "Other women's husbands hit them, at least you don't have a husband that hits you." I was gaslit into settling for the bare minimum: someone who went to work.

When I asked him to play with or somehow entertain the kids while I mowed the lawn because they were either crying for me or running in front of the mower, he bought me a riding mower so I could sit the kids on my lap while I mowed. When I remarked that I wasn't able to get everything done during the day and could he please help, he said it was because I spent too much time online, or that everything didn't need to be perfect.

I was told I asked for too much, but if the needs and requirements for running a household were being met, I wouldn't need to ask. I've been married before, I know how to run a house. I also know that it shouldn't require me to do it alone, or for it to be as much work as it was.

Research shows that even in dual income families, women do far more household and childrearing labor than their male partners. They also get less sleep and less leisure time. While this may be a "societal norm", it doesn't make it right. Women are blamed for creating so-called unreasonable standards for cleaning and raising children, and are then labeled as gatekeepers, preventing men from participating in these tasks. The gatekeeping is called such because our standards are typically higher than are men's, but if you look at it closely, they're not far-fetched standards just to make men's lives miserable.

When children are small, they need to be distracted, kept safe, and fed well. Just because you survived sticking a knife in a socket doesn't mean all children did. Just because you lived off junk food doesn't mean that's healthy. I used to drive home from clubs after drinking heavily, and I lived to tell about it, but that doesn't mean it was safe or smart. I could have killed myself or another. People like to joke that the warning labels on items are ridiculous, but just like laws and rules, they're there for a reason. Minimum standards of homekeeping and childrearing are like those ridiculous warning labels: someone is failing to follow them.

It should be obvious that if it takes two to create a child, a relationship and a marriage, it takes two to maintain it. Going to work every day is the bare minimum. Keeping your child alive is the bare minimum. Everyone in the family needs to be happy, healthy and thriving for a family unit to be successful. There is a right way to be a parent, and a right way to maintain a home.

The bare minimum for home upkeep is cleaning dirty dishes, otherwise roaches and bugs will appear. Keeping the floors swept, mopped and vacuumed keeps dust and dander, allergens and just plain nuisances, at bay. Cleaning the toilet keeps e coli from spraying in the air when you flush. Cutting up grapes and hot dogs isn't helicopter parenting, it's preventing a child from choking. Feeding a child healthy food isn't being snobbish, it's helping them to grow properly, that's just science, bro.

It wasn't that the goalposts were moving, it's that as the layers were stripped away, I was seeing each tree individually, and the forest was not being cared for.

~ 35 ~

I DON'T WANT TO KNOW THIS
MUCH IS TRUE | 2022

*On those mornings you struggle with getting up, keep this thought in
mind—I am awakening to the work of a human being. Why then am I
annoyed that I am going to do what I'm made for, the very things for
which I was put into this world? Or was I made for this, to snuggle under
the covers and keep warm? It's so pleasurable. Were you then made for
pleasure? In short, to be coddled or to exert yourself?*
~Marcus Aurelius

When I first read the book, *A Woman's Worth*, by Marianne
Williamson, in 1995, I was excited and hopeful for the future. I had
finally found a book and an author that inspired me that I could
accept and claim my power and truth. I savored every word, sitting
with a cup of peppermint tea, and often an alfajor, basking in the
thoughts of creating a new world where femininity wasn't weakness and society had promise.

I read it numerous times during the 90's, each time with fresh
eyes and anticipation. Once Jason graduated and we moved back to
Florida, it was my dream that I could host small groups of women,

129

creating a community where we would go out into our own worlds and exude love, kindness, feminine power, and change the world. I drew plans for what my facility would look like: an old house, full of rich fabrics and textures, a tree right in the middle, a room for art and creativity, another for yoga and massage, another for cooking fresh foods to be served, and walls full of books, with chairs thick and plush to sink into.

Unfortunately, my anxiety over feeling unsettled in our future led to restart my craving for cocaine, and I left Jason and our dreams.

I picked up the book yet again a few years later, and the hope and excitement I once felt had vanished. With this new relationship, there was no inspiration for a future filled with equality and divine feminine rising. It was, instead, a life with doldrums and seemingly endless drama, this time not directly caused by me.

My creativity was squelched. My passion for others was mocked. My desire to build community was met with accusations and insecurity. I shelved the book, only to pick it up once or twice in the next twenty years.

As I write this, I'm now a little over two months post-divorce, and I have opened the book again. The inspiration has returned, only this time with a daunting feeling looming overhead. Where once I felt empowered that even just my participation in the movement toward the divine feminine would create a ripple effect, now I feel like the work ahead is formidable, like slogging through deep mud. The hope is still there, but it's far off in the distance, and you can't make out what it is.

Just this week, fourteen children in Texas were slaughtered. Without getting into the disgraceful job the police officers did to save those children, it's excruciatingly painful to think of where we are as a society today. In 1995, we were still hopeful. In 2022, we are seemingly divided more than ever, and it feels like childbirth: a ripping open of our flaws as a country, as people; and it's bloody as hell. I feel such guilt and shame for burying my head in the sand for two decades, and even today, I feel guilt for laughing while children are being murdered, political parties are churlish against each other, Roe vs Wade is being gutted, and we are still talking about racism.

I want to feel hopeful again, but it seems far-fetched. I want to chase dreams of building a community where there is love and a passion for life and learning. I want to create again: art and words and pottery. I want to dance, laugh from my belly, and stand in the grass with the sunshine beaming on my face. I want to stare at stars and hear the crickets chirping. I want to hold hands with friends and lovers, and believe that the energy created in those bonds makes a difference.

I want to want all of this with every cell in my body, but it's impossible to recreate that stirring, knowing what I know. Knowing that there are people who don't want the best for you, even the ones you marry. Knowing that there are people who prioritize profits over people. Knowing that religion isn't about love or who Jesus really was. Knowing that there are men who don't really like women, just the warm soft place in our center that provides comfort for a few minutes. Knowing that our country, who proclaims to be the Land of the Free, really only wants control and domination for the most powerful and rich. Knowing that women are simply adornments, and not valuable contributors to society if we could just be heard.

Knowing that I have a daughter who has to live through this and learn these things, too.

When I again pick up the books I cherished and savored in my twenties, I am met with a feeling of disappointment in myself. Disappointment that I had a fire in my belly to elicit change, not only in myself, but in the community around me. Disappointment and fear that I may have missed the boat on my desired calling. Disappointment that so many years later, it seems as if the world around has gotten worse and I went along with it. The twenty years I spent going along to get along, setting aside my deepest beliefs and values, in order to have peace.

But the peace was an illusion. There was an internal war, yet I kept trying to suffocate the voice within. Telling myself that this way was the best way. Telling myself that outsiders knew better. Institutions that had been around for much longer than me had been doing it this way, and there was neither a need or a reason to try and do it any differently. Who was I to continue to buck the system, especially when those around me were content to remain in it?

My circle was small, and within it, there was an external war as well. Even though I was doing my best to play the game, it was as if I was just learning it, and the other players were pros. My body didn't know the movements, and I was running to the wrong bases, tagging the wrong player, or swinging at the wrong time. I was on the team, but I didn't fit in. Instead of deciding I was playing the wrong game for my skillset, I just practiced harder. I slowly began to bench myself, watching from the dugout, hoping to learn by observing.

At the same time, I am also met with a feeling of pride in myself. Pride for deciding it was time to sit on the bench and let the other players play their game.

The two decades I spent going along to get along wasn't all a waste. I realize this occasionally, but no time more predominantly than just early this morning, when my daughter texted me at 1:46 AM, asking to talk to me. Asking my advice. Trusting me with her thoughts. We had an hour-long text conversation talking about higher self and values and feminism.

This and other conversations with both of my kids would never happen if I hadn't benched myself. If I hadn't chosen to focus my attention on what was important during that time: creating and fostering relationships with my children. I chose them over everything else by always listening to their thoughts and opinions, lying in bed with them as they drifted off to sleep, talking to them about any and every little thing while we spent countless hours in the car, and mostly, by being honest.

Because if I failed my kids, I failed myself and everyone around me.

They didn't always know my plan was to eventually leave their dad, hell, I didn't even know it was my plan. I held onto hope that there would eventually come a shift either in him or myself, and suddenly the game would be so much easier, make sense. But what they did know was that I would always be honest with them. If I was struggling, I didn't make a huge deal about it, but if they asked, I would tell them the truth. If they wanted my opinion, I gave it to them as gracefully as I could. If I didn't have the answer for something, I would tell them, and we would research it together.

This isn't to say I was a perfect parent, no one is, not even parenting experts. But being a good parent isn't having all the answers or money or Instagram-worthy pictures. Being a good parent is accepting your flaws, and being human. Crying, messing up, and most especially, apologizing. Often. And with that apology, making sure to try to do better future forward. It gives them permission to screw up. It gives them examples of making amends. It shows them that it's perfectly okay to be human, fallible, and make mistakes. It's what you do with those mistakes that counts.

When I feel that twinge of disappointment that I could have been further along on my journey, that knot in my stomach that I wasted twenty years, and now I'm 50 almost back at the starting line, I look at my kids and recognize that time spent investing in them was never a waste. Even if I never have an audience beyond them, they're my most important audience. Because if I failed my kids, I failed myself and everyone around me. I could sell a million books or have the top-rated podcast in the nation, but if I don't have the trust and confidence of those I love the most, my kids, what's it all for?

Life is a journey, and just like any hiking trip, it's not linear. You zig-zag, and sometimes you even backtrack. Too often, we kick ourselves when we see where others are in their journey, because they're further along, or because from our vantage point, it looks as if we took the wrong or more difficult path. But if we step back for a moment, not competing, and observe the flowers, wildlife and trees along the way, incorporating them into our journeys, it makes the hike more memorable and enjoyable.

I could very well have taken steps along the way to be in a different place than I am today. I could have focused my attention on things that would have changed the outcome. And you know what would have happened? I would have wished I spent more time with my kids.

For me, personally, every mile I drove with them, every night I spent listening to their days' musings, every movie spent on repeat, every single minute I spent with my kids, was not a loss of time. If anything, those are both memories I treasure as well as time I would repeat in a heartbeat.

~ 36 ~

I KNOW THIS MUCH IS TRUE
| 2022

And forget not that the earth delights to feel your bare feet and the winds long to play with your hair.
~Khalil Gibran

I spent the first 50 years of my life waiting for someone else to step aside so I could have my time to shine. Waiting for my father to get sober. Waiting for my mom to leave my father. Waiting for my brother so I wouldn't worry about him. Waiting for someone, anyone to see me. Waiting for Jason to finish school and decide to settle in. Waiting for Karina to turn 18 so we wouldn't have the drama of her mother. Waiting for Doug to grow past his insecurities so we could live life. Waiting for him to trust me so I could feel free in myself again.

Waiting for God to answer my prayers to either make me stop wanting things that weren't important to everyone else in my life or to open their eyes up to allow me to be me.

What I know to be true is that all that waiting didn't produce the results I was waiting for.

What I know to be true is that sometimes you have to put yourself first, and if others think you're selfish or a bitch, or you should follow the rules, that's a they problem.

Because what I also know to be true is that when people are saying those things about you, they're actually putting themselves first. Their comfort. Their image. Their feelings. The things they're accusing you of, they're guilty of themselves.

What I know to be true is that you get one life, even if you get another one via reincarnation, you only get one life like this one. No matter if you believe that you go to heaven, hell, or get another form of life on earth, this personification, this embodiment you have today, is the only one you'll have.

The poem by Mary Oliver, "The Summer Day", is often summarized in one sentence, "...what will you do with your one wild and precious life?", and for many of us, we've misused it as a means of pushing us to do more, be more. It's not a poem of future planning, it's a poem of being fully present in the here and now.

I spent far too much of my life waiting for others to give me direction, to show me the way, to give me permission, to finish their work first. When X happens for them, then I can finally Y.

One thing I am ever-grateful that I held onto, my whole life, is being observant. After all this time, after all this life I've lived, the moon never fails to catch my eye. Sunsets never fail to cause me to smile. Babies never fail to make me want to hold them. Mistakes never fail to give me a lesson. Orion, my favorite constellation, never fails to make me say hello. My kids...never fail to make me grateful I kept going or thankful I stayed home with them so that I could observe them.

What I know to be true is that there is something beautiful in every day, if we are observant.

I know this much is true.

"...I do know how to pay attention, how to fall down
into the grass, how to kneel down in the grass,
how to be idle and blessed, how to stroll through the fields,

which is what I have been doing all day.
Tell me, what else should I have done?
Doesn't everything die at last, and too soon?
Tell me, what is it you plan to do
with your one wild and precious life?"
— Mary Oliver

~ 37 ~

EPILOGUE ~ HOME

You must train your intuition – you must trust the small voice inside
you which tells you exactly what to say, what to decide.
~Ingrid Bergman

I stand on the shoreline, my mind meeting my feet in a literal and ethereal space of in-between. The warm water kisses my toes, and I take in a deep breath of the briny air. The ocean is my home, and it's here, on the precipice between the soft yet sturdy sand and the deep vast unknown of the salt water, that I must make my choice once and for all.

To my left and my right are the two strongest women I've ever known: Jennifer to my right, and my daughter to my left. I look in my daughter's chocolate eyes and a small smile crosses her plush mouth. Jennifer reaches out and places her hand on my shoulder, her ever-present serenity passing through me as she inhales the air. A breeze passes over us, and I look behind me.

My mother, the one who brought me life, stands in the middle. Deep down, she knows why she is here, but that knowing hasn't reached her conscious mind. Next to her stands my dearest friend, Peggy. She knows, she knows. Our souls have been connected since the dawn of time, all of us. To the other side of my mother is my son, my firstborn. He is more evolved than my mother, and his knowing is present, but society and patriarchy are a constant battle for him.

On either side of the people behind me are the spirits of my grandmother and her sister, Gail, my great-aunt. Gail moves from her place to stand next to my grandmother, and reaches for her hand.

I turn back around to face the ocean.

So many choices I've made in my life, so many paths I've taken, mentally, emotionally and corporally. Until now, I've always known that if one path was incorrect, I could change the course. It wasn't always easy. People were hurt, disappointed and sometimes angry, including myself. But I've consistently seen that it worked out for the best for everyone involved.

Not this time. This time, there is no win-win. Someone comes out a loser.

My daughter takes my hand in hers. It's soft and warm, just like the day she was born. Her long fingers interlace in my short, thick ones, from years of doing massage. Helping others "get back to doing what they love" as my slogan was. The breeze pushes her long thick brown hair into my face. It smells sweet and sweaty.

My son steps up between Jennifer and me, and puts his arm around my waist. He's too tall to put his head on my shoulder, but he tries to, awkwardly.

The only sounds around us are the waves meeting the shoreline, some louder than others. The seagulls float in the sky above us, and the sun begins to lower.

Some choices you can't undo without causing a ripple effect that turns into a shockwave that destroys everything.

It's time. I grasp both of my children in my arms, tears streaming down our faces. They know this isn't the end, and yet, at the same time, it is.

"I love you guys, more than you'll ever comprehend," I tell them. "Do good, be good, and be good to YOU first".

A sob emanates from my throat. I feel it closing, like a golf ball is stuck in it.

I don't know what is on the other side of this, but it's the only answer I can find in all the years of questioning. A rebirth of sorts.

I step forward, slowly, into the water. Further out I go, and I force myself not to look back. The water laps around my waist, and I remember when my grandfather would stand with me while the waves tried to knock us over. I remember every year becoming more and more brave, venturing further into the deep waters while my grandmother called me back to shore.

A wave comes from my blindside, and takes me under. I break back through the surface, my bearings lost for a moment. I see the horizon, and another wave from the corner of my eye. I turn to face it.

It takes me deep underwater, where I'm from, where I feel oddly safe. I soften my body and let it do what it will to me.

I am *home*.

~ 38 ~

VOWS TO MYSELF

I will be both my own masculine and feminine,
My yin and my yang,
My husband and wife.
I will celebrate my victories, and hold my hand when I fall.
I will be my yes and my no,
My happy and my sad,
I will be my own soft place to land.
~s. kilata

ACKNOWLEDGEMENTS

My thanks to many people:

Douglas Hoekzema, aka Hoxxoh, the fantastically talented artist who painted the mural I used on my cover. This mural can be seen at 2130 Central Avenue, in St. Petersburg, Florida. It is an entranc-ing sight to be seen. He describes his work as wanting to "show us a different way of viewing time through a means of exploring its natural fabric."

Marianne Williamson, who has not an inkling in this world of who I am, but who has influenced so much of my life since her book fell into my hands in 1995.

My editor, Heidi, who laboriously pored over this work, gra-ciously overlooking my non-traditional writing style. I'm sure parts of this style gave her a headache, but still, she persisted.

The women at The High Rise, whose essence inspired me to finally hit "publish".

My friends and family, both online and in real life, who have supported me and cheered me on as I wrote this book, lost & found the manuscript, offered to "buy all the copies", and who have simply been there for me.

My (step)dad Art, who took on two bratty kids as his own. Who showed my mom that she is worthy of love.

My Momma. Oh, how I love you. Thank you for being my friend.

My Margeaux, who introduced me to Marianne Williamson's brilliant book, *A Woman's Worth*. It's been such a joy to learn with you in this lifetime.

My son, who marches to the beat of his own drum. Don't ever change.

My daughter, who has shown me the meaning of grace, and given me much insight into the world through her eyes.

My brother, who makes me laugh until my sides hurt, who tells the best stories, and who has a smile that lights up my day. If you don't have a brother like Mike, go out and find one. But you can't have mine.

~ 40 ~

PRAISE FOR I KNOW THIS MUCH IS TRUE

"This is a stunning soon to be released book. I think this is out-standing work and the type of story that should be shared, and in the current "climate," it might need to be a must read for organizations and leaders who deal with diversity issues every day." ~Calvin Lawrence, Ed.D, Motivational Speaker and Consultant

"This book is a must-read. She wears her journey of trials and tribulations like a badge of honor! She brings light, learning and healing to even the heaviest of topics. It's never too late to choose a new direction for yourself." ~Jenna Slaughter, Heart-Forward Business Coach, Speaker & Podcaster

"I love how the author describes her life in such a way that you feel you were there, too. There were some traumatic stories, but she tells them from a lens of healing. I was also in a narcissistic, emotionally manipulative relationship and it was affirming for me to read someone else's story, because too often, the events in these types of relationships are either hard to describe or swept under the rug. What isn't recognized is that it's the little events and emotional cuts that add up to feeling gaslit and confused." ~M. Stockwell

s. kilata found her love for writing at an early age, beginning with drawing pictures and having her beloved grandfather write the stories behind the pictures as she dictated them. She could be found, late into the night, reading by flashlight under the covers in her younger years. In high school, she discovered her style in Creative Writing classes, penning poems and later an entire high school drama series called "Anonymously Signed". It was so intriguing to other students that the hand written, loose-leaf paged book was passed around the campus. In her junior year, she applied for a scholarship at the Poynter Institute, and was immediately rejected. Although disappointing, she continued writing for herself for the next 10 years, until she discovered the author Marianne Williamson. From that moment on, she realized she had a story to tell.

I Know This Much is True is as much an autobiography as it is self-help, chronicling her tumultuous childhood years, melodramatic twenties, and losing herself in a one-sided marriage for the next two decades. Stepping out into her own voice, she discovers that within her, not outside, is where the true power lies.

Her compassion for others and the world around her, often to her own detriment, led her to practice mindfulness, even amidst the storms of life. She is a deep-thinker, an ally and fighter for the underdog, and her own unique outlook on life inspires others to claim their own authenticity and live that way more consistently. She hosts a podcast, The Suburban Misfit, facilitates online groups and women's book clubs.

She is the mother to three amazing children, a daughter, a sister, and one hell of a friend. She loves puppies, throwing compliments to random strangers, trolling fundamental Christians on Instagram, and swimming as far out into the ocean as possible. She plans to die fighting a shark.